The Jersey Death Squad:
A Journey to Kill Jessie Freeman

By Mark Meding

The Jersey Death Squad:

ISBN: 979-8324546434

CHAPTER 1 —

Shit happens.

What are ya gonna do?

Nothing', that's what I say.

Fuggedaboutit.

"Do nothing and everything is done," just to get all Zen about it. And that's what I would've done on my own—nothing. But others are involved. They have a say, I have to admit, and if they want to drive to Denver and kill our old friend, Jessie Freeman, who am I to argue? It's two against one, and this is still a democracy last I checked. Even in Jersey.

I own only one suitcase, which is plenty since I possess only four T-shirts, four pairs of boxers, two pairs of jeans, a couple of hoodies, an old and very cool leather jacket, and a half-dozen pair of workable socks. My wife, Angie, is always pestering me to buy new clothes—we got plenty of money—but I never saw the point. I do have a suit for weddings.

And funerals.

Mostly I wear sweats. A cliché, I know, but that's me all over.

All my toiletries fit into a large Ziplock bag.

I pack the suit, just in case.

I pull out my cell-phone.

"Hey, Gary, it's me, Scotty."

"I know, the phone told me it was you."

"Don't be a wise-ass. Are you gonna be a wise-ass for three days in the car, 'cause I'll kick you out five hundred miles from Podunk, Nebraska, swear to God. Now are you ready?"

"I'm ready," Gary tells me.

A lie. I can tell from his voice. The most unorganized slob in the history of unorganized slobs—

"I'm on my way," I say simply, and hang up. I don't bother to call Ian—it's no use. Ian was born ready.

"So that's it, then," Angie says, meeting me at the door to say goodbye. "You got everything—phone, meds?"

"All set."

"Phone charger?"

"In the bag."

"You'll call me, right?"

"Constantly," I assure her.

"Drive carefully."

"I will."

"Watch for ice on the bridges—they freeze up first, you know."

I chuckle. She always tells me that when I drive somewhere, even in the hottest summer weather. It's her way of saying "I love you and I'm going to miss you." Atleast I hope so. Angie's gorgeous, smart, and wonderful. She's the best thing I ever did. Her and the kids. I devoted my life to 'em and don't regret a minute of it.

I'm Scotty Carollo. No, I'm not Scottish. I don't even remember how I got that nickname. I'm Italian, to tell the truth. "Rudolpho Molero Carollo," but don't tell anybody. Call me Scotty.

I drive Argo, my Lincoln Navigator, to Gary's place. Gary Streeter lives in a funky part of town, Oakburgh's version of the East Village, which sounds pretty pathetic, and it is. Most of the residents of his building are in their sixties and beyond. Gary, at fifty-seven, is considered a youngster. And even though he's the same age as me and Ian and Jessup, we all consider him the "kid" of our foursome.

I pull up in front of the converted, subdivided brownstone and honk the horn. I'm not going in there—

likely to get a contact high on a vast range of airborne material.

I wait, annoyed out of habit; there's actually no hurry to get on the road. It's twenty-seven hours driving time, New Jersey to Denver, my phone tells me. We should fly; that would be the smart thing. But flights are hard to come by. The winter holidays are over but now it's ski season, record snow, and blizzards have cancelled a number of flights on top of it all.

So, I say sure, I'll drive.

"It'll give us a chance to reconnect," Gary pipes up, always the glass half full guy.

Or get on each others' nerves and kill each other, I counter in my head, *or get snowbound and have to eat each other's flesh to stay alive.*

Then there's money. Ian is rich as Croesus (ancient king—look him up), but I'm sure Gary doesn't have two nickels to rub together. I could offer to pay, or split it with Ian, but that would only embarrass everyone involved. *But it's okay we drive the Navigator, no matter what the operating costs,* I complain to myself. It's not a serious gripe. I complain, that's all.

Gary bounds down the steps, a worn army duffel over his shoulder. I have to grin. *The man loves life and doesn't mind showing it.*

"Hey, Scotty!" he announces, climbing into the passenger's seat. Once again, as I do every time I reconnect with Gary, I marvel at what unlikely friends we are. Raised by two gay men, both therapists, Gary had always been a free spirit, in love with life and everything about it, at one with Zen, yoga, Qigong, and "mindfulness," whatever the hell that is, not to mention massive quantities of weed and organic mind-altering substances.

"All ready to go?" I ask.

"Always," he chuckles.

Still a kid, and looks it, and acts like it.

"May Vishnu bless this journey," he states solemnly.

"You're not gonna light up a bunch of incense, are you?"

"I probably should."

"Not in my car, you aren't. No rain-dances, either."

"You're a real Philistine, you know that, Carollo?"

"Uh huh."

"You do know what that is, right?"

I know exactly what a Philistine is (I looked it up), but I don't reply. Instead, I hit the gas, spewing hydrocarbons into the air like the planet will go on forever. Alarm bells go off.

"Fasten your seatbelt," I tell Gary.

"Vishnu will protect—"

"The Lord helps those who help themselves," I shoot back, about as religious as I get.

Gary snickers, and buckles.

So, we bust each other's balls. It's all in fun (most of the time). The only place we never go (with Gary around) is making fun of the gay thing, on account of his two dads. There'd been awkward moments, and some tongue-biting, but we respected Gary just enough to tactly declare the subject off-limits. Not that Gary would've taken offense. He's the most peaceful guy you'll ever meet. Maybe not the most hygienic—already I get a whiff of unwashed armpits. And he's got a plastic bag of granola in his hands and he's tossing birdseed in his mouth, about half of it crumbing up Argo, which I get washed every week and detailed once a month, despite the ball-busting Angie gives me over it.

"Want some?" he asks, mouth full and open, bits of oat and raisin launched in my general direction as he aims the open bag at me.

"No thanks," I tell him, hoping I'm not hurting his feelings, 'cause despite the fact Gary can be a royal pain in the ass sometimes and a vast source of airborne particulates, everybody loves him. He's one of those rare, harmless souls who loves everyone and everything. How much was the drugs, who's to say? He took them all.

"Just for the experience," he explains when challenged on the subject. Back in school, he squeaked by only because his endless curiosity occasionally intersected with the subject-matter of the curriculum. He never had any aspirations for a career, college or anything with structure. After high school he becomes a Dead Head, following the Grateful Dead around, making a living selling food, Dead swag and drugs. He's a highly successful salesman, or at least he would have been if he'd been selling something more pricey than T-shirts and lids of grass. People look at Gary and see someone comfortable, like an old couch, someone they can confide in and curl up in and get warm. So, they tell him everything, all their secrets, their inner thoughts, and in the case of women, that kind of sharing usually leads to splitting bodily fluids, the little rascal. Nobody notices what I notice, at least at first: Gary himself never truly shares himself. For all his professed "free thinking" and "openness," the exchange is never quite equal; Gary holds back, keeping himself to himself. Of course that's from growing up with two fathers, a secret not too many know. But what am I, Sigmund Freud?

Now Ian, he's a different duck altogether. To see him is to know him, an open book. No deep waters there. He's Richie Rich, Daddy Warbucks, Scrooge McDuck. Okay, that's not fair. He doesn't act rich—he doesn't have to—he just is. Born into it, had it all his life. And he doesn't *look* rich. Skinny as hell, tall and awkward, he wears thick glasses. He's worn them as far back as I remember. Maybe that's why he never really gets into any fights. A guy might be willing

to knock your block off or bust your nose, but most are reluctant to hit a guy with glasses on.

Ian's parents are both still alive, and they live in Florida, or France, or Italy, or maybe all those places.

"We can't handle the New Jersey winters anymore," they claimed. "Just too brutal for us."

I doubt anything in their lives could be called "brutal." Ian inherited a beautiful home with a nicely manicured lawn and landscaping he pays someone to look after. It's a brick home with a brick-paver driveway. The inside is immaculate, too. His kitchen is all labeled with what belongs in what drawer and cabinet. His three-car garage has shelves that are neatly organized alongside his bike and workout gear, golf clubs, etc. His Mercedes sits inside the garage.

I bet he has his clothes all neatly stacked on his bed, ready to pack. Every move Ian makes is calculated and intentional. He still lives alone after his divorce; he's just wound too tight to have anyone else in his life. His house has great artwork his parents accumulated over a lifetime, which he guards like a mother hen but doesn't appreciate one bit. He has a home-office set-up where he buys and sells companies, and fixes them up—I don't know—what am I, an executive? His backyard is perfect for entertaining friends and clients, but he doesn't have any friends (Gary and me and Jess excepted), and whatever it is he does, it doesn't rely on wooing clients.

He marches out of his (parents') mansion with a couple matched suitcases, an overnight bag, a laptop case, skis and boots and poles, which Proctor, his (parents') aging butler, wheels out for him on a small handcart and loads into Argo's backside.

"Sure, you got everything?" I bug Ian as he jumps in the back.

"Cut it out."

"This isn't a vacation," I needle him.

"I thought there might be some time..." Ian replies sheepishly.

"Put on your seatbelt," Gary orders, "before speed-trap Bill here writes you up."

I smack Gary a short one, which he squawks at.

"That didn't hurt," I tell him.

"How do you know?" Gary comes back.

Ian belts up.

"Are we going, or what?" he wants to know.

"Aren't mummy and daddy gonna come out and kiss-kiss their baby goodbye," I reply.

"They're already there."

"Where?"

"In the Rockies. In Colorado."

"Jesus," I curse, "we're not meeting up with them, are we?"

"I thought there might be some time," Ian repeats.

Gary and I smirk.

"We have a house in Aspen. It's really quite nice."

Gary and I burst out laughing.

"C'mon, c'mon, let's go," Ian complains.

"Gentlemen, music," I announce, hitting the music and the gas at the same moment.

The Marshall Tucker band blasts on at ear-damage volume: "Can't You See?"

We're off.

CHAPTER 2 —

The night started typical enough with me calling Ian.

"Yo, ass-face!"

"Hey, fuck-head. What the fuck is going on?"

"Beats me," I told him. "What about you?"

"Ah, ya know, hangin' out, jerkin' it."

"Yeah, can you even find it?"

"What do you want, douche-face?" Ian asks.

"What do I *want?* I gotta have a *reason* to call now, Mr. High-and-Mighty?"

"That's right," Ian laughed. "I'm booked three months in advance."

"What's say we go out and get fucked up tonight."

"Lemme check my schedule."

It was Ian's turn to laugh.

"Yeah, man, let's fuckin' tear it up."

"Okay, ass-face. I'll ride up to your place at seven."

"What about Gary and Jess?" Ian asked.

"You know I called them first, before I settled on your sorry ass."

"Get outta here."

"Gary's out fucking a tree or something and Jess is climbing Everest. But I'll give them another call. If you get to those the dickheads before I do let them know we're going out to get wrecked. Make sure they don't have their periods or some bullshit."

"Got it, douche-bag."

"Douche-bags forever."

"Later, fuck-face."

It was 1985, the winter of our junior year of high school. Christmas was over and so was New Years. The days were just getting longer but the nights weren't any warmer yet. We were restless, like young bucks charging through the woods with reckless abandon. It was a Friday night. Jess, as always, wanted to go camping, despite the cold.

"We could freeze our nuts off out there," Gary complained.

"You'd have to find them first," Ian joked.

"I'm surprised your mother lets you out this late, Ian," Jess smirked.

Ian said nothing.

"Listen, I'm game to go camping if you guys are," Gary reversed positions.

"Hey, go ahead," I told them, but count me out. I ain't sleeping on the ground on the coldest night of the year."

That put a stop to that. Not that the other three ever listened to what I said, or that I was their leader or anything. I was just the biggest. Jess was our leader—good looking, naturally agile, a born outdoorsman, loved by the ladies. He was the brains, and I was the brawn, you could say. But that night the freezing cold won out over Jess's leadership. We stayed in town, and that has made all the difference, just to get all Robert Frost about it.

"The mall?" Jess suggested.

We grumbled. Fact was, at seventeen years of age, maybe we'd already outgrown the mall. Maybe even Oakburgh, New Jersey, entirely. Looking back, it wasn't perfect, but pretty darn close. You left the house in the morning—Saturdays and Sundays, summer and holidays—or after school, and hopped on your bike to go find your friends. You didn't come home until you either got hurt, got hungry, or the street lights came on. Sunday was dinner with family, which you never missed. If you were late you could hear your mom's voice calling out through the neighborhood, using all three of your names just to embarrass you. It was pretty sweet and innocent, on the surface at least, looking back, but at the time, to youngsters like us, who needed *something* to do, innocent or not, it seemed like a better place to be *from* than a place to actually grow up *in*.

"I thought the idea was to get some booze and some weed and get wasted," Ian complained, "then chill at the SpeedyMart"

I had to hand it to him—Ian tried, like it was some kind of original plan of action we hadn't acted on a hundred times the past year.

With no objection and no better ideas, we got on our bikes and headed through the center of town, the older part laid out with a Main Street and side-streets off it. We all knew how to drive but none of us was eighteen yet with a full driver's license, and by law weren't allowed to drive after nine p.m. or something like that if I remember right, except on "authorized farm errands" with our parents' permission, whatever those were, and hell, we weren't farmers. We were bike people, road hogs, street blasters, and our bikes were a big part of our identity.

Jess led the way, and on cue we executed wheelies halfway down the block.

Suddenly, Jess held up his hand and skidded to stop.

"Two o'clock," he whispered, nodding his head down the street.

I had to hand it to Jess; he had eyes.

Just poking out from a side-street, the tell-tale black and white shape of a patrol car. We hesitated. Not that we were breaking the law or anything, not yet—the night was young. No, the fear and excitement were an instinct, a reflex, a constant sensitivity to authority.

"Hello, boys!" a voice boomed out from behind us.

We jumped, we turned, we watched police officer Hank Polensky step out of the shadows like Freddy Krueger. We'd ridden right past him lurking in the darkness.

Officer Hank was both a friend and a threat. We liked him but he also made us nervous.

"Staying out of trouble?" he asked.

"Yessir," I replied for all of us, stepping forward. I knew my role, the Eddie Haskell of our little gang, sweet-talking authority, putting on the innocence and politeness.

Not that anyone believed it, but there was something about me (I was told) that put grownups at ease, and less suspicious. Little did they know.

"Scotty," Officer Hank smiled. "Your dad still on the street?"

Okay, so maybe Officer Hank *did* know.

"Of course," I told him.

"He still with the Teamsters?"

"Yeah," I told him.

My old man was a union officer, which made him a crook in people's minds.

"Whad'ya say his job was?"

"Consultant."

"Consultant about what?" Officer Hank needled.

"Labor relations," I said, which made the cop laugh.

"How 'bout you, Ian?" Hank turned to Ian. "You still wetting the bed?"

"That's not true," Ian shot back.

"You, Jess—you hear from your dad?"

"Sometimes."

"He still overseas?"

"I'm not at liberty to say," Jess answered.

"Good man, good man," Hank chuckled. "Loose lips sink ships."

"Yessir."

"We're all proud of him, you know," Officer Hank said sincerely.

"That's good to hear," Jess answered.

Jess's dad was in the Marines, on deployment somewhere—Granada, Middle East, South China Sea, Guam—we could never keep track.

"You tell him Officer Polensky said we're all proud of him—you got that?" Hank repeated.

"Got it—"

"But as for the rest of you bums—you keep your noses clean, understand?"

"Yessir," we answered, holding in the smirks, which he could see plain as day.

"I slept with every one of your mothers, you know," Polensky said, which weirded us out. When none of us laughed, things got even more awkward. "Just kiddin' you guys," he tried.

"Ha," I managed, trying to help him out, but it sounded like sarcasm, which made the others smirk.

"How about you, Carollo?" He turned to me. "You stayin' out o' trouble?"

"Yeah."

"Uh huh—that go for your dad, too?" he asked, going back to that.

"What'd'ya mean by that?" I asked.

"Nothin'," he answered. We both knew he was just talking, making conversation, killing time, bustin' my balls. He wasn't good at it—that was clear, the poor s*chmuck*. "Don't do anything I wouldn't do. But as for you—" he added quickly, arm shooting out at lightning speed, grabbing Gary's ear, squeezing hard, pulling him down to a half-squat, "—if I catch you with so much as an ounce of illegal substance, you're going to jail...*my* jail...and we'll just see how tough you are."

We stood there doing nothing. Hank was a police officer, after all, and could do anything he wanted. We didn't even have cellphones to record it all—that's how long ago that was. Officer Hank had a gun and a Billy-club and the badge of authority; we had nothing. But mainly we were pretty sure he was just messing with us—

"I'm just kiddin'," Hank smiled. "Get up, Gary." He *was* one of the boys, really, one of us, screwing around for kicks. If he had wanted, Hank could have easily busted us for real, and not only our balls. There was no doubt a felony or two in our pockets at any given moment, not to mention riding around at night on our bikes (serial numbers sanded off), without proper lights, without helmets, doing things that weren't exactly kosher, if you catch my drift. I won't specify—I was never entirely clear on that Statute of Limitations thing, and besides I don't want you thinking bad of me. Suffice it to say we usually never went so far as to get officially arrested, but even then, we figured we had a "get out of jail free" card in the person of Hank Polensky.

"I'll tell my dad you said hello," I told the policeman, pointing my bike toward the Speedy Mart. The others picked up on it and did the same, like we were in a big hurry to get somewhere to see someone important.

"Yeah, you boys run along," Hank said, like us riding away was *his* idea, not ours, waving his hand like a man shooing away a swarm of gnats.

After a couple blocks straight down Main, Hank's eyes on us the whole way, I hung a Louie down a dark alley toward McKinney, parallel with Main. We headed for Pete Bildorf's corner.

Pete Bildorf had graduated from high school five years earlier. He had never been college material and had failed at a half-dozen low-level jobs since. His only two skills turned out to be ground-level sales (dope) and being over twenty-one years of age. Besides weed, Pete sold pills when he could get hold of them.

"Prescription only," he boasted. "I don't mess with that street stuff."

He also sold beer to minors (us).

"But not the hard stuff, okay?" he'd say every time we asked. "You wanna get me in trouble?"

I skidded to a stop. Down the street, on Pete's corner, Pete himself was at that moment getting hassled by Iggy Barnes, high school senior, the town bully, and our constant nemesis, with a black heart and a violent bent.

"What the hell?" Ian hissed.

"It's a hold-up," Gary stated the obvious.

"We oughtta call the cops," Ian suggested, doubling down on the self-evident.

"Pete might get busted," Ian noted.

"Better than getting killed," I remarked.

"Where will we get our beer?" Gary worried. "And our dope."

"Iggy doesn't even have a gun," Jess pointed out.

It was true, but the steel bar Iggy was brandishing looked deadly enough.

"Why doesn't Pete just give him the money?" Ian wanted to know. "Or run."

Our instinct was to turn tail and take off on our bikes, wash our hands of the whole situation, but something just snapped in me the way it does sometimes—

"I'll get Hank!" Gary yelled, jumping on his bike, pedaling back the way we'd just come.

Good idea but too late, I remember thinking. I threw down my bike and started kicking cars like a crazy-ass donkey. Alarms came on, answered by other alarms, all up and down the block.

Jess, catching on, bravely but foolishly approached Iggy, attempting to distract him. Jess waved his arms wide, in a half crouch, the way a rodeo clown confuses a Brahma bull.

"Mooooo!" Jess called out, mocking, which caught Iggy's attention all right, and made him furious.

The siren on Hank's cruiser got louder and in a matter of seconds the vehicle careened around the corner, Jess following on his bike. Pete took off running. Officer Polensky let him go, all his attention on Iggy's angry, enormous hulk blasted white in the police prowler's headlights. Hank shut the siren off, stepped out of the vehicle and donned his officer's hat, the mantle of authority.

"What's going on, Iggy?" Hank Polensky asked calmly, like a trusted friend or sympathetic counselor.

"Fuck you!" Iggy yelled.

"Now, c'mon, Iggy, don't be that way. You having a bad night?"

All the while, Officer Hank kept approaching, a half-step at a time, hands up and in front of him, fingers wide.

"How about you just put that bar down and we talk about it? I can give you a ride home. Your mothers probably worried about you."

Hank was now ten feet from Iggy and the raised iron bar over Iggy's head, ready to swing.

"Stay there!" Iggy screamed like a cornered animal. We'd never heard anything so terrifying. Iggy had always seemed so self-assured when he was picking on people, never doubting himself or his ability to inflict pain at any moment. Where did this scared rat version of Iggy come from? Was it Hank's soothing, "community policing" tone of voice, or was it the mention of Iggy's mother?

Hank stopped where he was.

"You're in control here, Iggy."

Hank spoke so softly; we could barely hear him from our vantage point forty yards away—

Suddenly, Iggy swung the bar hard, releasing it at the last second. It flew straight from his hand to Hank's head at a terrifying velocity, glancing off Hank's upper arm, then smacking the policeman's temple with the sound of a skull cracking—a lucky shot, no two ways about it.

Officer Hank Polensky shivered like he was being electrocuted. His arms hung down, useless to break his fall. He went down hard to the pavement.

Amazingly, the police officer's paralysis cured my own. I charged forward.

Iggy's face contorted in agony. He hadn't meant to hurt Hank—that much his sorry mug told me. Iggy probably hadn't even meant to let go of the iron bar. Hank was a decent guy—even a miscreant like Iggy Barnes could see that—but now Iggy needed that iron bar back. I wasn't quite his height and weight, but I was close, and enraged as hell, murder in my eyes. I'd seen that look myself before (and many times since).

I scare people, I know that.

To my relief and disappointment, Iggy took off running.

I looked down at Officer Hank. He was out cold. If he was dead, I wasn't sure. It occurred to me to check his pulse, but I had no confidence I'd be able to tell, even with all the cop shows I'd seen. I left the iron bar where it was—that much my old man had taught me: "don't leave your prints at a crime scene."

A noise came from inside the patrol car.

"Hank? You there?" the dispatcher asked.

"Tell 'em," Jess urged and I realized my so-called friends—Jess, Ian and Gary—were standing right there straddling their bikes, too late to be of any real help.

"Answer," Ian chimed in.

I picked up the baseball-sized microphone dangling from the dash.

"Hello? Anybody there?" the dispatcher tried again.

I pressed the button with my thumb.

"Officer down," I said simply.

"Hank? Is that you?"

"Officer down," I repeated like a robot.

"Where?" the dispatcher asked.

I gave the names of the two cross-streets.

"What happened? Who are you? What happened?"

"No comment," I said. I didn't care what happened to Iggy Barnes but I wasn't going to be the one to rat him out. A guy could get killed that way, or get his mother killed, or his sister and brother—who knows how many generations? I released the button on the microphone and wiped it off with the tail of my shirt, suddenly trying to remember if I'd ever given them to any official authority. *Learner's permit?* I couldn't remember. "We better be going," I told my buddies.

CHAPTER 3 —

I drive. The music is down a little and the initial excitement of the open road has worn off. It's beautiful country, rural Pennsylvania, even in winter, *especially* in winter, you could say, brown and cold, with white patches of snow in places. Ian sits in the back keeping his mouth shut, thinking, no doubt, which worries me a little. He started out tapping on his phone but now he's graduated to a laptop plugged into the USB outlet, producing a weird, blue glow which I find distracting. I could ask him to cut it out, or move out of the line of sight of my rearview mirror, but I know it would start an argument, or a discussion, at least, which would then *lead* to an argument 'cause everything's an argument with these guys. For the time being I can live with the computer. At least no one's quarreling with the selection of tunes—classic rock 1965 to 1985—no disco, no rap. Not that I'm a racist or anything—I just never got it.

Gary, also uncharacteristically quiet, has his face buried in a well-worn paperback which is coming apart in his hands.

"You wanna know what I'm reading?" Gary asks.

"Not particularly," I answer.

"It's really interesting."

"Glad to hear it. Nice for you."

"You don't wanna know?"

"None of my business," I answer.

"Okay, suit yourself," he says with a sigh of disgust like I'd just hurt his feelings or something.

"Okay, I'll bite," I say. "What are you reading?"

Big mistake. Shoulda stayed out of it.

"*Blue Highways*," he says, "by William Least Heat-Moon."

"Yeah?"

"It's about traveling around the country and taking the back roads."

I can see where this is going, and I don't like it.

"The state roads that were there before the interstates," Gary goes on. "They're in blue on the map he has. That's where the title comes from."

"No," I state firmly, punching the button on the console, turning the music off. "We go straight to where we're going—"

"That's right," Ian chimes in from the back. "I got it all organized—the route we're taking, the filling stations along the way, possible eateries, rated for quality, price and convenience. Look, hotels—"

Ian tries to shove the laptop into the front seat to show us how it's all been mapped out. I elbow the computer back angrily, intent on breaking it.

"I just thought we could be a little bit more spontaneous," Gary protests. "Enjoy the journey, live in the moment, take the road less traveled by—"

"Thank you, Robert Frost," Ian smirks.

I laugh.

"*Fuck you*, Robert Frost," I add.

"We have to keep to the schedule," Ian explains, more of a question, really, to me, the tie-breaking vote. And although I agree with Ian about the route on principle, I also hate to be told what to do or where to go, or when, or how to get there.

"Okay, get this straight, you two jokers," I tell them. "We go Pennsylvania Turnpike, then to St. Louis, Kansas

City, then Denver. The fastest way possible, whatever the GPS tells us." I tap the screen on the dash, which is identical to the screen on Ian's laptop.

"That's all I'm saying," Ian says, retreating to the back, hurt.

"*My* GPS," I elucidate.

"Okay, okay," Gary answers,

"This is not a vacation. This is not a fieldtrip," I sum up.

I'm fifty-six years old, I got a wife and kids—I don't need to charge around the country looking for who-knows-what. Fuggedaboutit.

But I don't say that, not out loud. I've been feeling old lately, like some things are already out of reach, and some experiences I won't ever have. Ian and Gary don't have to know this. I'm reminded that despite the fact they're the same age as I am, they're still kids, really, same as I remember them back when, back when we were actually kids.

CHAPTER 4 —

The next day, after school, we went to see Officer Hank Polensky in the hospital. The story was on the local news, but there wasn't much information—no mention of Iggy Barnes or of four teenagers witnessing the attack. It killed us, this big event and we couldn't tell anyone we'd been there. We should have been famous, but we weren't. They said Hank was still alive but in critical condition. The mayor and the police chief offered "thoughts and prayers," blah blah blah.

"Family only, sorry," the nurse told us at the front desk. "And you gotta be eighteen."

"We're eighteen," I lied.

"Officer Hank's my uncle," Ian jumped in.

The nurse "harrumphed" her skepticism, but went ahead and added, "visiting hours posted here," absently pointing to a laminated notice on the desk. "Bring identification."

I went to work, the designated ambassador to the adult world, the sweet-talking emissary to the regular portion of the planet. I angled around the side of the high, circular desk so as to get closer to the ears of the middle-aged nurse. Meanwhile, Jess slipped around the other way to read the sheets of information—room assignments among them—taped to the desk—

"Ma'am," I cooed. "To be perfectly honest, we're not relatives exactly, just his best friends in all the world—"

She was already shaking her head, but that didn't matter—Jess was giving me a subtle nod and thumbs up.

"Well, thank you anyway," I said. "Have a nice day."

We were halfway down the hall when Jess whispered, "Room 102 C."

Instead of going out the exit door, we headed left down another hall with a last glimpse at the nurse who, fortunately, did not look up.

Intensive care was on the ground floor, next to the operating rooms, next to the Emergency Room, near the loading dock for the ambulances to pull into. Any idiot could have found it, room number or not, but we were young and stupid.

It wasn't what I expected—no large, private rooms. Instead, four patients, all unconscious, were laid out in beds surrounding a central console, each patient hooked up to a variety of tubes and wires. "C" was the designation of the third bed. It occurred to me that maybe the police department's health plan wasn't the best.

Beneath all the paraphernalia: Officer Hank Polensky.

We stared down at him for a while. The machines indicated he was alive, but you couldn't tell otherwise.

"Officer Hank," Gary said. "We're here to see you."

We all looked at Gary like he was looney-tunes. Gary held his hand up to tell us to be patient—he was going somewhere with this.

"I know you probably can't see us or hear us, but just in case," Gary went on, "we wanted to know we're with you all the way. You are not alone."

There was no response. A door opened behind us. We jumped.

"It's so good of you to come," said an attractive middle-aged woman holding a cardboard cup of vending-machine coffee. She looked at me first. "You must be Scotty," she said.

I didn't say.

"I'm Hank's wife. Teresa."

She held out her hand. I took it warm from the coffee. We shook.

A nurse came in and politely booted us out of the room. At Teresa's invitation, we sat in the waiting area to talk. To our surprise, Hank's wife knew all about us—Jess, Ian, Gary and me. She correctly guessed who was who just from Hank's description of us. It was a shock that Hank talked to anyone about us on his own time, particularly his wife.

"Hank always wanted kids," she explained at our stupefaction, "but we never could have them. I guess you guys were his kids, really."

We were all moved by that. In fact, Ian looked like he was gonna burst out bawling at any second.

"He saved our lives!" Ian declared. A lie, but well-intentioned, but which could get us all in trouble, both with the law and with Iggy Barnes and the avenging hordes I imagined Iggy Barnes could summon at a moment's notice.

I glared at Ian, then warned the others, too, with a look.

"Last night? You were there?" Teresa Polensky asked, checking all our faces.

To my amazement and relief, nobody—not even Ian or Gary—gave anything away.

"Some other time," Ian backtracked. "He saved us another time. On an earlier occasion."

Should've left it alone, I thought. Clearly, Teresa wasn't buying it.

"They said it was a kid named Iggy Barnes," she said, her eyes again darting between the four of us.

“The high- school bully," she added. Again, none of us indicated weknew a thing about it. "Somebody called it in."

Nobody moved a muscle. We could've won an Academy Award.

Who called it in? I wondered. Again, blank stares. *Remind me never to play poker with you guys,* I thought to myself.

"They took the boy into custody," Hank's wife went on. "This morning," she concluded.

CHAPTER 5 —

As I drive west into the falling sun, dimly glowing through the hazy clouds of a frozen sky, I think about the quickening aging process. I recall my mom and pop at that age and wonder if they felt the same. Frankly, I doubt they were capable of any introspection at all.

My parents, both gone now, were old-school, second-generation Italian. Mom stayed home and busted us kids' asses—me, my older sister Carolyn, and my little brother, Danny. I say she busted our asses, but she didn't spare herself, either. Dinner was on the table at five-thirty, and the house was spotless. Pop worked for the Teamsters—at least that's what he claimed. He was a wannabe mafia mobster, you could say, but if he ever busted any actual skulls, I don't know—and I ain't talkin'. All I know is he regularly came home with items that "fell off of the back of the truck."

When I was younger, I took that literally and whenever I'd see a truck I'd keep an eye on the rear end to see what would happen. I figured there had to be some gimmick to it. How the big rear door of a truck could pop open and dump fur coats and boom boxes and designer shoes was beyond me, particularly since most of the truck doors had big honking padlocks.

So yeah, maybe Pop was not such a solid citizen, but he was a lovable guy behind the superficial toughness. He demanded respect, I'll tell you that. It was his favorite word: "Respect." And he loved his family more than anything in the world and would do anything for them, larceny included.

I try to focus on the road. Gary's still reading his book in the dimming light. Ian, in back, has fallen asleep. I've got the music on low, and I figure I have another hour or two of driving in me. I've decided not to let Gary or Ian drive the Argo—not yet anyway. Both are good drivers, though Ian could be nervous behind the wheel, and Gary was maybe *too* relaxed. I turn the music off.

"Maybe we should stop and eat," I say to Gary quietly.

"Yeah, I'm hungry," he answers. "Where are we?"

"We're getting close to Wheeling, West Virginia," I tell him. "The sun's going down and there might be ice and sleet and snow in the mountains. We need gas anyway, so maybe we should eat and figure out a place to stay the night and make a reservation."

"Sounds good," Gary agrees, marking his place in the book and tucking it in the side-pocket of the door, surprising me—no objections, no snide remarks, no nothing. I'm bewildered. Everything is changing. Just when I think life is a straight line from birth to death, along comes Jess and this Colorado thing, indicating life is more of a circle or a spiral or a helix doubling back on itself. And Gary has changed, or maybe I've changed.

Ian hasn't changed. He snores in the back, mocking me.

"Let Ian use his computer," Gary whispers softly. "Let him pick the motel and the gas station."

I start to say something snide. I let it go. Maybe I'm losing my snark; I don't know.

"Okay," I say.

CHAPTER 6 —

After three days of looking, the state police found Iggy Barnes and arrested him. He hadn't gone far, just a couple towns over, holed up at a cousin's house. They took him into custody without a fight, and he confessed to hitting Officer Polensky with the iron bar, though he claimed it was an accident and he hadn't meant to hurt anybody, which may have been the case, or maybe not. I was right there watching the whole thing and I couldn't tell. I gave up trying to figure what's in people's minds a long time ago. I don't know what's in my own mind half the time. There was no mention of a local drug dealer or four teenaged witnesses to the whole thing. We watched the local news on TV every night and read the paper each morning but there was no hint as to who made the call, or how they got Iggy Barnes' name to begin with.

Among ourselves, nobody asked the question. All I knew was that it wasn't me who'd dropped the dime on Iggy Barnes, and I could live with that.

For his part, Iggy never ratted us out to the authorities, or to his lawyer for that matter. As screwed up as Iggy was, I think he was still smart enough to know our testimony wouldn't do him any good.

The four of us—Gary, Ian, Jess and me—got invited over to Hank's house by his wife, Mrs. Polensky. She was nice to us, and it seemed like she didn't want to be alone, so we went. She was attractive in a middle-aged woman kinda way, and I know we all had "Letters to Penthouse" fantasies about her, but mostly we felt sorry for her, and when it snowed, we shoveled it off her driveway and walkway, and after it rained we cleared the leaves out of her gutters.

We also went to see Hank with her. His condition hadn't changed at all. It was a tough thing to contemplate that he'd be a vegetable for the rest of his life. Eventually he'd die, of course, but that could take years, the doctors said.

It was stressful and uncertain, and one day Mrs. Polensky broke down in intensive care, dropping to her knees suddenly, wailing, bawling, a gushing outburst completely out of character for her. We stood there without a clue what to do. There was a red call-button next to Hank's pale-white hand on the hospital bed, as if Hank was going to wake up and summon a nurse to bring him a plastic cup of orange juice.

Gary started to reach for the button. I grabbed his wrist and shook my head ever-so-slightly, warning him not to. I guessed it would be an embarrassment to Hank's wife to have the nurses rush in and find her on the floor, overcome with grief. Still, none of us wanted to touch her and hold her, fearing she'd let out that scream again.

Finally, as the designated liaison to the adult world, I reached down to her. She took my hand I pulled her up the way I'd help a fellow basketball player who'd fallen on the court. Suddenly she grabbed me around the neck and back and held me tight and cried into my chest, since I was several inches taller. She was petite, I realized, not the pillar of strength we'd thought she was, and I was desperate to protect her from every danger. And I also thought impure thoughts.

We guided her back out to the waiting room—the five of us together now like a rugby scrum. We sat her down at the round Formica table and Ian hurried to the men's room for a stack of paper towels to dry Mrs. Polensky's tears.

She thanked us and apologized to us for making such a scene. We didn't have an answer for that. We couldn't reassure her, we couldn't say "there, there." We weren't old enough for that, and it would be overstepping to forgive her or tell her we understood, though both things were mostly truc.

We went to the woods. We always did that when things at home or in town or at school got too complicated and confusing. Pete, our dealer, disappeared after that night, but somehow, we managed to scrounge a bottle of Southern Comfort and a bag of weed. The weather had warmed up a little. We hiked into an area called The Pines, a section of 1000 acres that was mostly Pine Trees. We set up camp at one of our favorite spots. Jess led the way like he always did.

"Someday we're going to map out this whole creek area," Jess had vowed a year before. "Every little bend in the water, every rise and bluff."

It sounded like work to us, but we didn't say anything. The woods for us was a place to get away and be ourselves and safely get drunk and high and use all the curse words we couldn't say aloud, but which desperately needed to be said since those words so precisely described the darkness of our souls.

"This is just a preliminary sketch," Jess had explained, carefully unfolding a large sheet of paper and spreading it over a large, flat rock. We could see he'd already penciled in much of the creek. "After I get my surveyor's equipment and I learn a few more things, we can really do this up right."

We nodded and agreed—Gary, Ian and me—though the idea seemed a little weird to us—geeky, in fact.

Jess was a true outdoorsman. He loved camping, hiking, skiing, rock climbing and ice climbing. He loved being in the woods and felt truly connected to nature. Jess got this from his father, who was a Special Forces Marine, busy invading Grenada or engaging in small skirmishes—Libya, Iraq, South America. We didn't know where exactly top secret and all that.

Jess was a great student and very popular. Everyone liked Jess. The jocks, burnouts, preppies, geeks and brainiacs all loved him. He judged no one and respected everyone. He was the first one there to help if you needed help. He stood up for the kids that would get bullied or picked on but stood up for them in a way that even the bully wouldn’t mind. He saw people for what they were and believed in them.

He could have done anything he wanted in life, but Jess’s greatest aspiration was to work outdoors.

"It’s the only place I'm truly free," he had said once with such sincerity we didn't even smirk or bust his balls about it. When Jessup’s father was home on leave, he and Jessup would disappear into the wilderness and the older man would show Jess how to live off the land. Jess's father's affection for Jess was the silent, frozen kind, matching his rigid, marine-like approach to everything. I could see he loved his family, but I also figured he saw too much on his assignments for him to really connect with anyone. Jessup was closer to his mom who was a loving person, very nurturing and a marine’s wife. She walked on eggshells when Jess's father was home and seemed relieved when the soldier went back out on assignment. She was a school nurse at the public high school we all went to, a fact Jess tried to keep secret. She was always around to be there for Jessup, which annoyed him more than comforted him, it seemed to me. Jessup's father sent all his pay home and when he was home, he was out hunting, living off the land and bringing home game to freeze for the family to eat.

That night, we stared at the fire and smoked and drank the booze, saying nothing except "Man," "Fuck," and "Shit."

Eventually, we got more articulate: "Can you believe it?" "Son of a Bitch." "Mother Fuck."

"Did you see how she collapsed on the floor?" Gary asked rhetorically. "I've never seen anything like that."

"I have," Ian said.

"Yeah," Jess agreed.

I didn't comment. The fact was, I'd been just as freaked out as Gary had been—not something I'd admit to any of them.

"We oughtta pull the plug on him," Ian said.

Nobody said anything. I didn't think Ian was serious—

"You're right," Jess agreed suddenly. "We should."

"I agree," Gary chimed in. "Put him out of his misery."

I didn't say a thing. I looked at their faces, flickering orange from the fire. Devils are what they looked like, scheming from the depths of Hell. Maybe it was my Catholic upbringing or maybe it was because I couldn't imagine Officer Hank Polensky with that crooked grin of his wanting anything except every last second of life he could have, coma or no coma. I thought of his wife, Mrs. Polensky. Teresa was her name, but I would never call her that to her face. *What would she do without him?* In a coma or not, he was still on this Earth—

"None of our business," I spoke up. "We're not his family. We don't have a say."

The guys shook their heads and clucked their tongues. They wouldn't disagree with me, not openly, and not on something this important. They knew that underneath all the joking around, I was a hothead, capable of violence, which made me angry.

"His wife won't do it," Gary commented.

"No, she won't," Ian agreed.

"Women," Gary muttered in disgust, which made me smile. *What did Gary know about women?*

"I wouldn't put my family through that," Jess said with some vehemence.

"But would they pull the plug on you?" Gary asked.

Jess shook his head—he didn't know.

"My parents would get their lawyer to do it," Ian smirked. "And *he'd* probably just hire someone else."

"My dads wouldn't do it," Gary stated, "no matter how bad it got." Which startled us. Gary had never said "dads" before. He'd say "parents" sometimes, which jarred us a little, since we knew he meant two *men*, but never "dads." He stared into the fire, thinking about them while Jess and Ian traded looks with me—they'd noticed, too.

"We need a backup plan," Jess decided, standing. "If one of us gets brain-dead, we need a plan so the rest of us can pull the plug."

Me, I wasn't so sure. I loved life. *A lot.* I mean that. And if there was any chance of squeezing a few more seconds out of this crazy existence, no matter what the circumstances, I was ready to go for it.

The idea embarrassed me, but it was three against one and I didn't want to be the odd man out. At that age, you go along. Peer pressure, they call it now; back then it was just the way it was. These were my brothers, after all. We were that close.

"Okay, I agree," I shrugged. I didn't want to make trouble. I could see they considered this a test of our friendship, Jess especially. Besides, what were the chances of it happening the way Jess laid it out? "I'm in," I added, secure in the knowledge that nothing would come of it.

CHAPTER 7 —

"Jess is in a coma," Ian tells me on the phone.

"What?"

"He's in a coma."

Ian gets the news first. I don't do the internet much and neither does Gary. But Ian's on social media or a chatroom or something—I don't know. Somebody's told the group Jess was involved in a ski accident. He's in a coma in a hospital in Denver.

I call Gary.

It's not that we lost touch with Jess. We still see him every year or every other year, usually at Christmas when he'd come home sometimes. Fall was a good possibility, too, a slow period for the travel/vacation business. He'd gone west after high school and worked for almost thirty years as a ski instructor in the winter and as a rafting guide in the summer. It sounded like a wonderful life to us.

"Bet he gets all kinds of pussy," Ian comments every time the subject comes up.

"Bet he does," Ian agrees.

I gotta say I'm envious, too. But then again, I have Angie.

Sometime around the time we all turn fifty, Jess quits the ski-slopes and rubber rafts and becomes a full-time Park Ranger. That much we know, and the fact he had a wife, then got divorced.

"We gotta get together and figure this out," Ian says that night, urgency in his voice.

"I guess," I reply, more of a sigh, really. Ian remembers that night, that's obvious. I wished he didn't.

Gary remembers, too.

We all remember.

We meet at the Beehive, a solidly average local establishment with nothing much to recommend it except the drinks come cheap and quick and they let you sit there forever, which we often did. By all rights we should have gathered in the pine woods where we met those nights after Hank's attack. But that place was long gone, the trees clear-cut to make way for a housing development of modest-priced homes (then, overpriced now). New trees were planted, one for each front yard, one for each in back. The new trees are fully grown, but no resemblance to the past remains—only in our memories.

"Is he really in a coma?" I ask, maybe for the third time on my fourth beer.

"That's what they say," Ian confirms. "Just like Jess laid it out that night. He's on life-support. He's a burden."

"How do we know that?" I protest. "Do we even know if his parents are still alive?" I ask.

The other two don't have an answer.

"They moved away at some point," Gary says. "To a warmer climate, I think."

"I can search on the internet," Ian says hopefully, pulling out his phone, fumbling with it.

"We know Jess got divorced."

"Does he have a second wife, a girlfriend? Kids?" I press.

Again, no answer. Ian plays with his phone, but the bar's too dark and Ian's eyes are too old to see.

"This is crazy," I tell them, putting my hand over Ian's screen. "I'm not running off to mercy-kill somebody on the basis of nothing."

"It's what he wanted," Gary speaks sincerely, soberly.

"Thirty-nine years ago," I shoot back. "Maybe he changed his mind."

"Jess would never change his mind—not about that," Ian states.

"Okay, I'm not talking to either of you 'til you have another beer," I proclaim.

Maybe they should put that on a mug, I think.

Gary smiles a sarcastic smile and waves in the direction of the bartender.

"I've had enough," Ian says.

"I mean, things have changed," I try. "There are like advanced directives and shit. I had to sign one in the hospital before they'd even fix my hernia."

"When was that?" Ian asks.

"Couple years ago. You remember."

"I thought that was a dick enlargement."

Gary laughs.

"Ha ha, you two."

"Well, did you sign it?" Ian asks.

"Sign what?" I ask.

"Permission to kill you."

"None of your business," I reply. Actually, I lied—it hadn't been required. I didn’t sign it. I didn't say one way or another. If it came to it, Angie would have to decide—I remembered that much.

"So, what did they do?" Gary asks, speech a little slurry. Maybe he's had enough, too. "Make it longer *and* bigger around? Length *and* girth?"

"Cut it out."

"'Cause I think most women would like it wider," Gary goes on, "but figure what's the point of getting their cervix all pounded to hell?"

Ian finds this hilarious. He and Gary can't stop laughing.

"Grow up," I tell them.

"Well, at least he died doing what he loved," Gary states.

"What, falling down a mountain?" I ask.

"Skiing," Gary says.

"He was never the type you'd see sitting at a desk," Ian recalls.

"Or working at a warehouse," Gary adds, a dig at me, I suppose. That's what I do, work in a warehouse. Making sure shit comes in and shit goes out. Loading trucks and unloading trucks. Getting shit moving. Like a large intestine. Like my Old Man. Waste of life, I suppose.

"He was where he needed to be," Gary says like some sort of Zen master.

"Away from here," Ian snickers.

"He loved nature," Gary concludes.

"But then nature killed him, didn't it?" I remark.

"Fuck you," Gary says.

"Yeah, get out o' here," Ian agrees.

I laugh.

They shake their soft, squishy little heads. I take another big swallow of beer to wash down the nausea.

CHAPTER 8 —

Jess and I went first. Since it was Jess's idea, he made the rules.

"Okay, we kneel before the fire," he told me.

I did as he asked.

"You, too," he told Gary and Ian.

They did it without comment.

"Now we look into each other's eyes," Jesse said.

"Do we hold hands?" Ian asked, breaking the tension.

Gary laughed.

"Yes, actually," Jesse said, the earnestness breathtaking.

I could see he was serious about this, and as corny as it was, I had already decided to go along, if only to preserve the friendships in the group. Gary deserved that much. We shook hands, the "bro shake," ready to arm-wrestle.

"Now repeat after me."

Though my memory is highly suspect in most circumstances, I recall the exact words Jess made up on the spot, and I particularly remember the yellow-orange red in Jess's eyes as he made them up, a reflection of the fire, no doubt, but also indicative of the burning in his soul. We swore to each other that "no matter what. we will honor this pact, even if it includes murder."

The fire popped and crackled in response, which sent a religious charge up my ass.

"If any of us are for any reason physically or mentally debilitated..." Jess went on, leaving a space for Ian to make some smart-ass remark about Gary's mental ability—a space Ian left alone in testament to the solemnity we were all feeling. "...and unable to care for ourselves, live free or be a burden to family or friends, the others will do what they can to let him die with dignity.

We all agreed. That was 1985.

CHAPTER 9 —

Now it's 2024. Are we different now? Maybe. Maybe not. Do people really change or are we the same poor slobs from the minute we're born to the day we die?

Take Gary for instance. Please. Rim-shot.

It's dark already. He's got the map-light on and he's buried in his book. He missed a spectacular sunset and now he's missing a crisp, cool night with the car-lights from the opposite direction dancing over the blackness of the pavement and across the windshield. He's reading a book about taking the scenic routes. Missing it all.

You'd expect a guy like Gary would turn out different, which he did, what with the two male parents and all. To begin with, he's just as interested in girls and women as the rest of us—let's get that straight, pun intended, ha ha. And you'd expect he'd be a bit of a free thinker, which he was.

But mostly Gary just loves The Dead. Can't explain it. Gets hooked on 'em in high school, and as soon as he graduates, he asks the dads for money for a van so he can chase that band all over the continent. The dads go for it, chuckling about how they'd once "sowed their own wild oats" back in the day, but mostly they don't want their precious son driving an unsafe wreck, or hitchhiking. They're a bit snobbish about buses and trains, too, so they buy Gary a brand-new mini-van which Gary junks up with a mattress for a bed and a bucket for a toilet. Gary further embarrasses his dads (designers, graphic artists, in the ad business) by slapping Dead stickers all over the exterior as well.

Gary puts down the book and shuts off the map-light.

"Wow, what a night," he observes. "Beautiful, isn't it?"

I agree, but the words choke in my throat. Suddenly I feel like I'm gonna cry or something, it's so beautiful, and I know it won't last forever. I'm pushing sixty, my parents have been swallowed up by the retirement monster, and even people my age—like Jess for instance, maybe—are leaving this Earth. It chokes me up a little. We aren't guaranteed tomorrow—

Ian pops up from the back seat like Jason Voorhees. Gary screams.

"What the fuckety fuck, fuckface?" I cry out, getting control of the vehicle again.

"Asshole," Gary mutters.

"You girls wet your panties or something?" Ian grins.

"Fuck off," I tell him.

"There's a recommended motel thirty miles up the road," he informs us.

"Well, as long as it's fucking 'recommended,'" I say.

I pull into a filling station. I figure we might make it to the motel, but we'd have to get gas first thing the next day anyway.

Ian goes into the little market to pay for the gas and look for snacks, drinks, beer. Gary goes around the back of the building to smoke some weed. Who knows what state we're in or what the laws are here.

Long way to Colorado, mountain high.

I start to fill up when I hear a sort of plop sound around front, so I go to see what that is and it's a guy with a pickup in front of me and he's got the gas nozzle in his hand, and I see that he's carelessly flung gasoline all over the hood of

Argo. I say "all over"—it's only a tablespoon or two, but it's the principal of the thing, right?

"Hey, there—look what you did," I order, maybe with more anger than the situation merited, but then again—

"What?" he laughs. "That's nothin'. It's just a car, dude—chill out."

Which makes me all the more angry. His pickup, which looks like it's never been washed in its entire existence, might be "just a pickup," but the Argo—

Let's just say I come from a long line of Teamsters, and we don't treat our vehicles that way.

He's a kid, really, just out of high school if he ever got that far. I figure I can beat the crap out of him with one hand tied behind my back and teach him some manners at the same time.

"Look," he says, demonstrating with the nozzle, waving it around, "the thing's got a leak," and proceeds to fling gasoline all over the place, most especially on my Navigator, which turns my burner up to boiling. He laughs again, bordering on hysteria. I know right then that no thickness of Turtle Wax (and I lay it on thick, believe me, no lie—fuck the cost) is gonna protect my precious Argo from the corrosive petro-carbons in that shit, but what am I, a chemist?

"You wipe that off!" I command him.

"Yeah, right," he says sarcastically. "Whatever. After you kiss my ass, grandpa."

Stupefied by anger, The Hulk comes to life, I charge, swinging with my right—standard haymaker, The Widowmaker, tried and true, nothing fancy—

"Yeoh!" I scream, a sudden pain in my shoulder knifing down my back.

"You okay, old man?" the punk asks me as I struggle to stay upright, holding onto Argo's front fender.

I charge again—forget the bad arm, forget the pain—wrapping myself around the jerk, prepared to slam him against the gas-pump, but now it's my other shoulder, and my back again, and my breath, which I can't catch to beat the band.

When's the last time you worked out? my mind wants to know. *I mean seriously, a really intense workout? Or been in a fight?*

He laughs, holding his ground—

"You wanna dance with me, pops?"

—and he's still got the gas-nozzle in his hand, ten pounds of solid steel, which he taps "upside my head" as the kids say these days. Residual pain from an old root-canal shoots across my skull to my bad ear (from two fights back), which rings like a cowbell.

"You're a dead man, fucker!" I shout, but it comes out all weak and raspy. I suck in air but it's not enough. I start to cough. "I've beat up assholes twice your size," I say without conviction, suddenly aware of an old hernia, right side, clearly torn again.

"You and what army?" he quips easily.

Without him even touching me again, I go down hard, face planting SMACK on the filthy, oily, grime-infested, gray-black cement surface of the filling station.

The co-pay on this is gonna be murder, I'm certain.

He laughs again, which puts me into an even hotter rage. I reach down and around, trying to grasp something, a weapon of some sort. *Am I so dazed I think I have a gun on me, or a knife?* Just my keys, *but that'll do*, I think, *if I go for the eyes or the throat—*

"Think fast!" the punk shouts, swinging his leg, steel-toed work-boot aimed at my skull. It's a glancing blow, denting the Argo, and now I've got that piled onto the pain: "failure to protect the vehicle guilty as charged."

One more time I try to rise, but the history of a few dozen fights, even stretched over a lifetime, plus the routine ailments of aging, prevents it. My mortgage flashes before my very eyes. A leak in the roof, the busted garage-door opener, the drippy bathroom sink. My life is a massive two-ton, book-length to-do list weighing down on my shoulders.

My opponent, on the other hand, carries few scars, few worries, no obligations. With one swipe of his hand, the youngster yanks my keys from me. I know instantly he's got me by the balls; without the fancy high-tech, theft-resistant key-fob, there's no way I'll get Argo going again, not without an emergency house-call from an authorized Ford dealer and a court order from a federal judge.

My ridiculousness mocks me, my throbbing, obligation-addled brain taunts me. I don't know whether to laugh or cry. I'm thinking, "Scotty, you never lost a fight," which isn't entirely true, and then there's my dad in my brain saying, "Well, there's always a first time for everything," which is something he said, usually right before violating one of society's norms.

The scream of a banshee fills the night. I recognize it immediately: Gary's high screech, the marijuana-fueled sound of outrage, straight from the bowels of Hell, transgender, racially neutral, as diverse as blood, as equitable as death, as inclusive as murder. Something had come of all those years gyrating to The Dead, this *dance macabre*, a work of performance art charging out from behind the filling station's little shop-and-go.

Gary leaps and screams and twirls, a whirling dervish, arms and legs going in and out and around and over in a dizzying pattern, a dazzling pace, kung fu on LSD, something beyond antiquity, before prehistoric, something primeval.

Like an endless Jerry Garcia solo—

The punk, to his credit—fundamental, ancestral terror kicking in—recognizes the scene in front of him is not of this physical world—who hits who, who inflicts pain, who suffers it. This is into the Other, past fear and desire, the Spirit World come to take revenge on all that is unholy. This is church, not the gutter.

The young man drops the gasoline nozzle, and my keys.

Yet he cannot move.

Gary, too, freezes on the other side of the SUV, the one called Argo. The hiss of a devil-wind fills the vacuum. Gary's eyes dart insanely, searching for a weapon, a worldly hard/sharp tool to add to his godly arsenal. He reaches for the windshield wiper.

No, not the windshield wiper, I whimper to myself.

Too late; Gary's already broken it off, and he's whipping the air with it, making it sing like the deadly fangs of the sacred asp.

The punk, eyes wide with terror, scoots around to the driver's side of his pickup, jumps in, starts it up and careens from the station, door slamming shut only after he's gone.

"You okay?" Gary asks like a regular human being again, back from whatever dimension he was in.

"I'm okay," I lie. I'm not okay. My head hurts, my shoulder hurts, my back and hips hurt, and I can't be sure of my ability to win a simple fistfight, let alone a brawl. Then there's my teeth, and that hernia. "I'm okay," I repeat. But I'm not okay. I'm not the man I once was, and Gary knows it.

"Ian's coming," Gary tells me.

"Lemma get in," I say in panic. I don't want Ian to see me this way.

"Get in the back," Gary says as he helps me in. "I'll drive." He picks up the keys.

Ian arrives with a big bag of various unhealthy snacks and a couple of six-packs of beer.

Gary jumps behind the wheel.

Ian sizes me up, bloody and bruised in the back of the vehicle.

"What happened?" he asks.

"Nothin'," Gary and I both tell him together in two-part harmony.

"Drive," I say.

"Buckle up," Gary answers.

CHAPTER 10 —

The first time we saw Officer Hank Polensky was when we were just fourteen maybe, and he was new to the force. The four of us—me, Jess, Ian and Gary—rode our bikes out to "the old highway," which ran past "the old orchard." I say orchard, but it wasn't more than an acre or two of unkempt, untended trees. The place had been abandoned, and if you got there at the right time—late summer, early fall—you could have your pick of apples. But we mostly got there later—end of October—when the half-rotting fruit on the ground was more to our purposes. Hiding behind the tall weeds on the shoulder of the highway, we'd launch those apples skyward, way up, like a quarterback throwing a Hail Mary bomb to a wide receiver in the end zone. The object of the game was to hit a car down the road—seven points for nailing a windshield, three for anywhere else on the car, ten points for a shot into a convertible with the top down, though in October that was a rarity. We considered it good, clean fun since we stuck strictly to rotten, mushy apples which wouldn't break glass (so we believed). The drivers truly didn't know what hit 'em since we threw from behind them, safely hidden in the weeds.

"Cops!" Jess shouted out, indicating a black and white patrol car coming our way. Jess grabbed his bike. Ian and Gary jumped on theirs, too, and followed the sound of their wide, knobby tires making squishy sounds as they rode over the rotting apples.

I didn't run. I could see the vehicle was moving quickly, not trolling for youthful apple-throwers, and I had other ideas. I scooted along behind the wall of weeds, hands to the ground, searching for the perfect apple—decomposed enough to make a putrid mess on a windshield but solid enough to fly high, straight and true. I spotted a good reddish-brown apple just in time and grabbed it the same moment I heard the patrol car whoosh by at the speed limit. I rose tall, took aim—not a second to lose—and let the apple fly with all my muscle, a monumental throw, far beyond my personal best.

As if in slow-motion, the orb finished its upward arc and descended, accelerating, miraculously on target—

"Holy fuck," I hissed to myself.

SPLAAT!

The sound from down the road was massive, wet and repulsive, but I didn't have a chance to savor it because it was quickly followed by the screech of tires and squeal of brakes.

Officer Hank Polensky was out of the vehicle in an instant and scanning for the culprit.

I ducked down, hoping he hadn't seen me. I was a big kid with a giant mop of reddish hair, easy to recognize. I looked into the orchard, where Ian and Jess and Gary had stopped. They'd heard the SPLAAT too, and the screeching tires, and had looked around to look, but just for a second. Having surmised what had happened, the little cowards jumped on their bikes and started peddling again, abandoning me there.

I rolled down a small slope, slipping behind a tree. My bike was too far off—I was better off leaving it. I wasn't wearing a jacket—big mistake. I took my shirt off—it had wide orange horizontal stripes—easily spotted, like prison garb. If Polensky had seen me, that's what he'd recognize.

Then I ran. Behind me I could hear a police car taking after me, onto the shoulder. There was a fence, but it had fallen into disrepair, and would be no match for the LTD if the driver wanted to follow me into the orchard.

He did. I dodged left and right, around the trees, a pattern I hoped would be impossible for the car to maneuver. It was the 80s, heyday of Pac-Man, and I'd played far more than my share. In retrospect, it wasn't a fair fight. The orchard's trees were just far enough apart for the big prowler to make it through, but turning ninety degrees in the full-sized vehicle was impossible at any speed.

You're beat, sucker, I gloated, slowing my pace. *I am a ghost. I am Blinky, the fastest ghost!*

But then I heard sirens. Soon there would be police cars everywhere. This was a law-and-order town; apple heavers weren't tolerated. I made for the woods, where the cop-cars couldn't go.

But what if they had dogs?

"Hey, Scotty!" came a whispered cry.

It was Ian, peeking out from behind a tree. Gary had hidden behind another one.

"Don't say my name," I admonished, going to them.

"What happened?" Gary asked.

"He chased me into the orchard," I told him.

"In his car?"

"Yeah," I answered. "He didn't have a chance."

The sirens were getting louder.

"We need to get outta here," Ian advised.

"Brilliant, Einstein."

"It sounds like there's an all-points bulletin out," Gary noted.

"Where's Jess?" I asked, suddenly aware he wasn't there.

Ian and Gary looked at each other, embarrassed.

"He went home," Ian said.

"Home?"

"He said he had to get home," Gary corroborated.

"Chickened out?" I asked, appalled at the thought.

Ian and Gary just shrugged—they didn't want to say.

"Let's go get him," I said, "and beat the crap out of him."

We ran, the other two pushing their bikes—the ground in the woods was too uncertain, too thick with leaves. I needed to get a shirt on. The cops would spot me for sure—the only guy running around New Jersey in late October without a shirt on, let alone a jacket.

The woods ran up right to Jess's backyard. There was a chain-link fence, but the gate was never locked. We could see Jess's bike on the ground near the back door. Past the house, we could see the street—no flashing lights, no staked-out police squad.

"Leave your bikes," I told Gary and Ian. "On three, we make a run for it. One, two—"

I ran, never getting to three, like I always did, jumping the gun, getting a head start, cheating.

We ran up the back steps to Jess's house and into the kitchen without knocking, which wasn't unusual—Jess's mom and dad treated us like family.

"Hello guys," Mrs. Freeman greeted us. She'd been washing dishes and was now enjoying a cup of coffee and leaning casually against the sink. She was a lovely woman, and we all had thoughts about her. She always had a dress on, and an apron it seemed like, with her hair done up high on her head.

"Hello, Mrs. Freeman," I said, suddenly remembering I was the Adult Ambassador, then recalling a second later I was naked from the waist up. Instinctively I stood taller, better to display my abs and pectorals— My face blushed red.

"Jess is upstairs," Mrs. Freeman said with a smile.

We ran, charging up the stairs and into Jess's room—the door was unlocked.

But Jess wasn't there.

Sounds caught our ears—a faint whimper, shoes on wood. Gary went straight to the source, the closet, and jerked it open. We all expected the C.H.U.D. monster to leap out, but it was just Jess curled up on the floor of the closet whimpering, shivering with fear, a sight so disturbing none of us made fun of him, and I even lost all desire to beat him to a pulp—

"Think fast!" Mrs. Freeman called from the door, tossing something as she walked past in the hall, headed back to the kitchen. Gary had shut the closet door—Jess's mom hadn't seen Jess. I held up the T-shirt, which said USMC on it, which obviously belonged to Jess's father, big enough for me—nothing Jess owned would have fit. I treated it as a gift, and it filled me with a sudden joy, intimate and personal. Somehow Jess's mother had sized up the situation, and come up with a solution. I wondered just how much she knew about us, and how much she knew about the trouble we and her son got into. Had she been listening to us just now?

I put the shirt on. I sidled up to the closed closet door.

"Hey, douchebag," I said.

"Yeah, jerk-head?" came a brave whimper back.

"Catch you later," I told him, signaling the others that we were leaving. "Bye, Mrs. F," I said to Jess's mother on the way out through the kitchen.

"Take it easy, guys," she said.

CHAPTER 11 —

Ian wants to call the cops.

"No," I tell him firmly. "No cops."

"The guy hit you with a gas-pump, right?"

"No cops," I repeat.

"I should drive you to an emergency room," Gary says, trying to look me over in the rear-view mirror from the driver's seat, which he adjusts with the little buzzing buttons, forward and higher to fit his smaller frame.

"No doctors, either" I tell him. That's pride talking, I know. Nobody has to know I lost a fight. And then there are the other issues—hernia, teeth, back, shoulder, hips. "They'll have me in a fucking wheelchair screaming for Saint Raphael."

"Who?" Ian asks.

"Saint Raphael the Archangel, patron saint of healing—don't you pussies know anything?"

"I'm Jewish," Gary states.

Ian laughs.

"No, you're not," I contradict Gary. "To be Jewish, your mother would have to be Jewish, and you don't have a mother, do you?"

Silence ensues.

"Just two fucking dads," I add.

Gary, clearly agitated, shifts in his seat, still trying to catch me in the mirror, but I'm a slippery little bugger—

"Keep your eyes on the road, willya?" Ian complains.

"Obviously," Gary seethes, "I have a mother."

"Yeah? What's her name?" I reply. I really don't want to have this conversation. I'm angry, that's all, and need to hurt someone. The fact Gary just saved my life makes him the ideal target.

"Listen, asshole—" Gary croaks.

"C'mon, guys—" Ian tries, but he has no influence whatsoever here. "Look, a motel."

So, we stay the night, no further discussion about religion or Gary's birthmother (who remains a mystery). It's two adjoining rooms with a door between them, what the sunken-eyed motel manager calls a "swoot." It's not on any of Ian's lists, recommended or not. In the interest of peace, Gary gets the solo room; me and Ian stay in the other one. There's an ice-machine next to the office. I drink a beer, press ice to my face, nurse my wounds and watch some old movie on broadcast TV. I think about calling my insurance company about the damage to the Argo. I decide against it.

Ian works the computer—the motel has wi-fi, apparently, surprisingly. Ian goes to the door to the next room and knocks. Gary answers.

"Okay, if we're still in Pennsylvania," Ian says, referring to the laptop, "it's not legal, but it's decriminalized. If we're in West Virginia, same thing. Not legal again until Ohio, and I don't think we're there yet."

"Thanks," Gary says. "I think I'll chance it. Want some?"

He produces a joint, like magic.

Ian shakes his head.

Gary looks at me—a peace offering.

I shake my head, holding up my beer, indicating I'll stick to that.

CHAPTER 12 —

It was a party. That's all we needed to know. And we were going, hell or high water. It never occurred to us it would be mostly seniors, with cars, or their parents' cars, or carpooling, or in taxis, but we were only fifteen, dependent on our bikes. We didn't care that it was miles away, or that we hadn't been invited. It was a party.

And we were drunk as hell.

Except the party was at the top of a high hill. It started as a slow climb, then it gradually got steeper. Jess made it a challenge, pumping and huffing ahead of us. My legs were done-for, but I wouldn't admit it. Ian's bike—a ten-speed, of course, store-bought and paid-for—was more capable of making it. Ian pedaled and pedaled at a ridiculous rate, which made a silly whirring sound, forward-moving, eventually overtaking Jess, at the expense of Ian's legs and lungs, but by the looks of it—

"None of us is going to that stupid-ass party!" I proclaimed, getting off my bike and looking up at the mountain rising ahead of us. I'd be damned if I was going to walk my bike all the way up that hill. ("People who walk their bikes are wusses," I'd always declared.)

Gary dropped his bike in the middle of the road, staggered over to a nearby flowerbed and promptly barfed up, making a grotesque sound which we all echoed sarcastically in our own way, which we found hilarious, which it was, believe me.

"That's it, enjoy the party douchebags," I told them, turning my bike back down the hill.

"We will!" Jess declared. I started to coast back down. At the last second I took a side street, just to see where it went (which made all the difference).

A few minutes later, I was headed back up the hill behind the wheel of a 1983 Cutlass Supreme.

"You kids need a ride?" I asked casually as I drove up beside them.

"What the fuck?" Gary proclaimed.

"What the fuck is that?" Ian embellished.

"It's a car, dumbass," Jess concluded.

"So, get the fuck in," I told them.

They hid their bikes in some bushes. I'd stashed mine in a hedge around the corner. Then I drove us all up the hill...in style.

Still drunk as hell.

"I didn't know you knew how to hot-wire a car," Gary gushed.

"Lots of things you don't know about me," I crowed mysteriously.

Ian laughed.

"Yeah, what's the big joke?" I asked.

"You are," Jess replied from the backseat. I swung to hit him, missed, hit Ian instead, which was okay by me, but when I swung a second time, I hit Gary, who hadn't really done anything except start the conversation with his stupid "hot-wire" observation. Truth, was I found a car with an open door and the keys right there in the ignition. Not too bad if I say so myself, considering that like the others I was still drunk as hell.

The party? Don't remember it at all, except there was no booze and no girls our age. The girl whose house it was at hadn't mentioned to her parents (as happened sometimes back then) that she was hosting a get-together and was surprised by the number of guests and party-crashers—not just us—who showed up, to the point where she ended up calling the cops *on her own damn party!* Fortunately for us, we got wind of the police coming, piled into the Cutlass and hit the road. We stayed low and drove slowly and managed not to break out laughing as we passed Officer Hank Polensky driving up the hill in the opposite direction towards "the scene of the crime."

The only other ramification was that in order to steer clear of the police, we had to park a mile away from where we left our bikes. We abandoned the Olds with the doors open and the keys in it in an industrial park parking lot, no worse for wear. If you're reading this and you owned that car, now you know the mystery of that little joyride it took one night. We didn't dent it or throw up in it, which was kind of a miracle considering we were drunk as hell. So you're welcome.

CHAPTER 13 —

I drive in a lot of pain, but mostly my ego is bruised, and there's no cure for that. It's raining, too, adding insult to injury, and I'm missing a wiper on the passenger's side thanks to Gary ripping it off in the heat of battle. So okay, I can see okay with one wiper going if it doesn't rain much harder or turn to sleet or snow or hail. We need to stop anyway—I never got any gas the night before, despite the fact Ian had paid for it.

We'll get a new wiper somewhere, I assure myself.

"You didn't get gas?" Ian asks.

"There was a fight," I remind him. "The gas never got in the tank."

"Jeez," Ian declares, like this is an affront to all that's holy. He gets on his cell-phone and his computer to get the gas station's number. He calls his credit card company—

That's when it happens, straight out of a book or a movie, my Old Man slapping me in the face all the way from Boca. We're somewhere in the middle of Indiana, I think. The road's a little rough. Well, not a little rough, more like the surface of Jupiter, and you can bet there's some politician in the state capital bragging about how low Indiana's taxes are—cause and effect, *ipso facto.* So, we're bouncing around like Beyoncé's butt in her latest video, and the wind's blowing like that girl in high school—you know the one. Argo's up for it, no problem, but there are a couple of box trucks ahead of us who've slowed to 60 mph or something and are swaying pretty good one way and the other, threatening to go over or off the road. I start to signal to go around when the truck ahead beats me to it, darting out into the passing lane without signaling, or maybe the driver's completely lost control—hard to tell. It's a rental truck, probably some slob kicked out of his house, moving on to the next town where they don't know what a poor slob he is, so I give him some slack and merely tell him to fuck himself under my breath, refraining from any hand gestures. After all, the thing's a rental, and the last time the driver drove a truck was probably *never*.

Okay, *now* is when it happens. The truck hits a pothole or a boulder or some kind of F.O.D.(Foreign Object Debris—that's what we called it in the service) and the back door snaps off the latch and the roll-up door flies up. Inside are the entire belongings of the poor slob—TVs, furniture, a treadmill, power tools, bedsteads—all bouncing right at the Argo, cracking the windshield, crunching tires and undercarriage.

I'm swearing holy vengeance and trying to keep the Navigator under control, all the while amazed how prescient my Old Man had been.

"Fell off the back of a truck," he's saying, and I'm laughing like a lunatic—finally this poor slob of a moving-truck driver had made an honest man of Pops.

"What the fuck?' Ian and Gary want to know, more disturbed by my hysterical laughter than our near-death experience. I pull over to the shoulder and watch as the truck keeps on going, still spewing F.O.D., driver completely unaware his personal belongings are littering the interstate.

"It's always amusing when figures of speech turn into truth, ain't it?" I comment to Gary and Ian. We're sitting on the side of the highway, the rain coming down harder now, seeping through the cracked windshield, and I don't seem to be upset one bit. "Ever see pigs fly?" I ask them.

I catch Ian catching Gary's eye. Ian's twirling his finger around his ear and Gary's nodding slightly, certain I've got brain-damage.

I just laugh.

CHAPTER 14 —

We referred to it as The Summer of 48. Forever. Not 1948, of course, none of us are that old. The 48 referred to something else—I'll get to that.

In fact, if I remember correctly, which sometimes happens (save the brain-damage cracks, please), it was the summer after the school year when I stole my first car and drove us up to the party at the top of the hill. It was Saturday and we started the day off at Ian Mathers house. I say "house", but it was really something of a mansion, with tons of rooms, lots of bathrooms, and "grounds" big enough to play baseball or football or soccer or whatever the hell you wanted to. We did none of that, preferring to "hang," "shoot the shit," and other vague occupations. Ian's house had a tennis court and a swimming pool, too, just to finish painting the scene.

Ian's mother was drop-dead gorgeous, the way rich people are sometimes. A stay-at-home mom, she wasn't ever too far away from us, even when we gathered at the far reaches of the property. She'd be ready on the spot with cookies, brownies, sodas or anything we wanted—the perfect hostess. I wondered what she'd say if I asked for a beer or a Scotch or a bag of weed, or twenty minutes with her in one of those bedrooms.

According to Ian, his mother hadn't always been so uptight and afraid of everything.

"She was once a wild child," Ian confided to us at some point, "but then she met my father..." Ian trailed off, shaking his head.

"Yeah, then what happened?" I asked, genuinely interested. In fact—maybe you noticed—I had a pretty strong and unhealthy interest in all my friends' moms.

"She turned into what he wanted her to be," Ian concluded.

"Huh," I replied, my mind trying to grasp that concept, wondering if it was such a bad thing to be what your man wanted you to be. I wondered if a girl (woman!) would ever like me that much to do that for me.

"Is that why you're such a chicken-shit?" Gary asked Ian, to which Ian replied with a swing of his hand, after which a slap-fight broke out for a minute or two, and we were all juveniles again, for the time being.

Ian's old man was a Professor at Rutgers, he was always ready to tell you.

"Professor Mathers," he'd introduce himself like he was too fucking smart to have a first name. Rigid? You bet—like with a broomstick up his ass. The man had the stink of money about him, too, like teaching college was a hobby, somewhere between stamp collecting and breeding polo ponies.

Ian's mother, the former wild child, Leslie Ann Mathers, came from money, too—you could tell. She sure didn't need to work outside the mansion, and she didn't. If she'd been a rebel and a hippie, that was all gone now; she was more "beat down" than beatnik, really.

Gary had been kidding about what made Ian so chicken-shit, but the truth was Mrs. Mathers' high-functioning anxiety was a lifestyle she imparted to Ian. It's no wonder he turned out the way he did with the parents he had.

"Let's go shoot some hoops," Ian jumped up. There was a basket set up at the end of the tennis court, but that wasn't the one Ian had in mind. He wanted to go elsewhere, to the public court, weeds shooting up from the cracks in the cement.

This time, maybe because of the conversation we'd just had, nobody busted his balls about it. He wanted to get away from his house, no matter how nice it seemed to the rest of us.

The basketball court was just a few blocks from my house, in an older, red-brick part of town, right next to an Italian/Greek restaurant where my family went to eat a couple times a month, and where the Old Man hung out sometimes during the day.

We were playing a little two-on-two—me and Gary on one side, Ian and Jess on the other. It was a fair pairing—

Jess was the best player; I was the tallest. Ian and Gary were eager but devoid of skills, and clueless as far as court sense was concerned.

A liquor truck pulled up to the back door of the restaurant. The driver got out of the truck with a clipboard in hand. He knocked at the back door. The owner, Gus, let the delivery man in.

I casually bounced the ball to Jess, an idea forming in my head. I wandered off the court.

"Hey, what are you doing?" Gary wanted to know.

I held my hand up and put my other hand over my mouth for them to be quiet. I walked around the chain-link fence that separated the basketball court from the restaurant and went to the back door, which was now unlocked. I went in.

The storage room was pleasantly cold, but also dark. I picked up the first case of booze I could see and headed for the slit of light that delineated the back door. As quietly as I could, I backed out into the sunlight. Only then did I look down to see what I'd taken.

Banana de menth! An entire case of the stuff. I resisted the urge to barf.

Gary, Ian and Jess stood hanging on the fence, waiting to see my next move. To their surprise, I made a U-turn and walked right back into the building.

"What are you doing?" Jess hissed in a loud stage-whisper.

I put the case of banana piss back where I found it and picked up another case. I didn't dare turn on a light, even if I could've found the switch, and remember, that was before everybody had a phone with a flashlight in their pocket. I could hear Gus and the truck driver talking up front, in Italian, I think, or maybe it was Greek. What am I, a linguist? (A cunning linguist maybe, ha ha.) Any second they'd be walking to the back storeroom to talk liquor and shit. I had to take whatever was in my hands and pretend to like it.

"Rhubarb schnapps, my favorite," I'd tell the guys, and choke it down like mother's milk if I had to. Booze is booze, after all.

Once outside, I skipped quickly past the basketball court and down the street. The others trailed me like the Pied Piper's rats. Anybody watching could tell by our faces and body language we were committing a felony.

"Stay cool, you dumb ducks," I hissed at 'em.

Gary reached for the wooden case.

"Leave it alone," I warned him.

Which didn't work.

He pulled a bottle from the case.

"Whoa!" he exclaimed.

Then the others had to look.

"Seagram's 7 Crown," Ian enthused. "That's big-time."

Congratulations followed, and pats on the back, but nobody offered to carry the case for me, which was getting pretty damn heavy. When we finally got the booze to my house and had snuck into my room, we counted 48 half-pints of the whisky.

"Jackpot!" Jess pumped his fist.

"Epic," Ian joined in.

"I declare this the greatest summer of all," Gary crowed. He grabbed a bottle, unscrewed the top and took a short, painful swig. "The Summer of 48!"

One of the finer days of my life, you could say. One for the history books.

After we hid the bottles in the wall-space at the back of my closet—a secret safe I had designed and constructed for just this kind of purpose—we walked back to the basketball court for our bikes, shooting a few hoops just to establish an alibi if we needed it.

CHAPTER 15 —

The Argo is in bad shape. Besides the windshield, there's other front-end damage and the two rear tires are toast. A quick glance tells me the suspension's fucked: a tie-rod and some bushings, but what am I, an auto mechanic?

I manage to get AAA on the phone and with the help of a mileage marker, am able to tell him where we are. He says it'll be two hours. I ask him politely to try to get to us sooner; he says he'll try. Everything's polite and caring and "please" and "thank you," which I'm not used to, which makes me a little nauseous.

Ian insists we use the time to take pictures of the damage to the vehicle and shots of the broken belongings strewn everywhere. He's sure I'm going to need documentation of the accident for the insurance company and maybe a suit against the truck rental company for a defective rear roll-up door. He seems to know what he's talking about. As a rich person, from a family of rich people, he knows a lot about lawsuits and lawyers and insurance and courtrooms and litigation, I figure—the stuff I've tried to avoid all my life, a genetic disposition, you could say.

Gary, meanwhile, using his foot like a broom, sweeps debris off the highway as best he can, scurrying to the shoulder when cars whiz by thanklessly, unaware how much money Gary has saved them (risking his own life) in tire costs and repair bills.

My life is Foreign Object Debris, lemme tell ya.

When the tow-truck driver shows up—a tall, skinny kid with a new ball-cap with the name and logo of a tractor company I'd never heard of—he takes one look at my face and insists on calling an ambulance.

"No, no ambulance," I tell him.

"But you're hurt. You got injuries," he points out, looking to Gary and Ian for support, and perhaps wondering why they escaped unscathed. I see he also notices the airbag hasn't been deployed.

Meanwhile, I hear Ian's mind churning around, thinking up some insurance angle, no doubt. He's still got his phone-camera in hand; he's itching to take some shots of my purple-bruised face and fold them into the mother of all lawsuits.

"From a previous incident," I tell the kid.

"Shoulda seen the other guy," Gary chimes in, helpful as always (sarcasm).

The kid gasps.

"A fight?" he breathes, turning his head back to me in shock, all the blood leaving his face. He's certain he's come across three armed and dangerous criminals, the kind of guys who willy-nilly get into ballroom brawls.

Raising his hands, moving slowly, apologizing—he's seen shit like this in the movies—he goes to the tow-truck and retrieves a clipboard and pen, then apologizes some more as he asks for my auto-club card and writes down my license number.

New Jersey, I see him thinking. It occurs to me he hasn't asked what happened. I hadn't said anything over the phone, and he hadn't asked driving up. In the space to explain "service reason," he writes only "road debris, busted windshield, etc."

CHAPTER 16 —

The next day after the orchard incident, early in the morning, I snuck back through the apple trees on the lookout for cops. It occurred to me they might stake out the scene of the crime just in case any fugitive fruit-throwers decided to return, which is exactly what I was doing. It was worth the risk, I figured, to get my bike back, and then there was the matter of that orange-and-white shirt which I'd left behind, which might be tied to me via DNA—I'd worn that shirt way too many times in a row. The kids at school, or maybe one of the teachers might identify it and rat me out. The possibility the police wouldn't go to that kind of trouble to nab a rotten-apple thrower never crossed my mind.

The bike was right where I left it. So was my shirt.

It's a trap, I decided, staying some distance away, staking out the site for fifteen or twenty minutes to be sure. Finally, with no sign of any law enforcement activity, I screwed up my courage and dashed to my bike. I hopped on and rode to the shirt, reaching down and scooping it up stunt-rider style, racing through the orchard, slaloming around the trees, stuffing the orange-striped shirt under my flannel shirt. That should have been the end of it but leave it to me—out of the frying pan and into the fire.

CHAPTER 17 —

We consider checking into a motel outside of the small town where the Argo's getting fixed. The place is not inviting.

"We should keep going," Gary urges.

"Great idea, Einstein," I tell him. "You want to walk, or you plan to flap your wings and fly?"

"We can hitchhike," he says. I see he's serious—though romantically delusional, imagining himself a character in a Jack Kerouac novel—

"Absolutely not," I answer. "Who's gonna pick up three middle-aged men out here in the middle of nowhere."

"We look like prison escapees," Ian agrees.

"We could hop a freight."

I laugh. Ian joins me.

"What?" Gary demands to know. "We promised Jess—"

"When's the last time you jumped onto a freight train?" I ask Gary. "Wait—don't answer. I know already. The last time you hopped a freight was *never*."

Gary sighs. I'm right. Bingo.

"We could take a bus, or a passenger train," Gary says softly.

"And leave the Argo?" I ask. I don't tell them how much I hate bus stations and train stations. It's been forty years since I've been inside one, but I remember well the cigarette butts embedded in the piss-sticky floors and the smell of people's lonesome poverty. Part of its snobbery, I know, inherited from The Old Man, who prided himself on never having to stoop to public transportation, for whom the ownership of wheels was a badge of manhood.

"Or we could rent a car and drive it to Denver," Gary suggests, "then pick up your SUV on the way back, after it's been fixed."

It's a good plan, but I'm not too keen on the idea.

"I'll pay for it," Ian says on seeing my hesitation.

It's not the money, but I don't tell them that. I let them think it's my unholy attachment to my oversized vehicle.

It's not that, either.

The truth is I'm scared. They don't know how scared I am, and I don't feel like "sharing."

Shit happens, you know. What are ya gonna do? Fuggedaboutit. We're only a day's drive from home, but that means one day closer to Denver, a place I want to avoid right then. The other two have it down—where we're going, what we're going to do when we get there. Me, I'm not so sure.

"Kill Jess." I know there's more to it than that. I know it's a good deed, exactly what we promised, out of love for each other. But I got qualms, okay? I mean I've done things before, horrible things, but not that.

"It's what we promised to do," Gary states out loud.

So he gets that I'm scared. So what?

"I'm staying right here with the car," I tell them. "You guys do whatever you want to do."

I'll do it—chicken out. Go yellow. I don't care. Let them go on by themselves. I'll turn tail and run back to Oakburgh. Come up with some family crisis with Angie or one of the kids. So, what if they see right through me? Let 'em call me chicken-shit. I don't care. I got nothing to prove. I've proven myself to them a hundred times, haven't I? I'll beat the crap out of 'em both if I have to. In fact, they're both overdue.

As I watch Ian and Gary give each other a look, I feel my hands clench into fists, first right, then left. *Give 'em the haymaker I should've given the pickup guy in the filling station.*

We stayed in Indiana. We checked into the motel.

"Let's get shit-faced," Gary suggests.

I laugh—Gary's answer to everything. Suddenly, I love them both again, their predictability and transparency.

"Good idea," Ian agrees.

CHAPTER 18 —

I rode to school with that orange-and-white-striped T-shirt wadded up and stuffed under my regular shirt. A couple wags in the hall punched at it, asking if I've put on weight.

"Pregnant," they decided, laughing.

I let it go. I needed to get to my locker and bury the shirt under the pile of debris there before somebody connected it with me and the rotten-apple fiasco, then I had to figure out how to smuggle it out of school ASAP. Locker searches were rampant in those days, privacy be damned.

"Yeah, well maybe you should just go fuck yourself!" I heard Iggy Barnes yelling at some poor slob. Iggy and his victim appeared from around the corner, the victim with a tenuous six-foot lead, walking quickly, not a run yet—

Iggy stopped at his locker, prepared to finish this later—

"Asshole," I heard from down the corridor, the victim daring this one last word—

That did it. Iggy slammed down his backpack and took off after the poor kid, scrambling out of sight down another hallway.

A crazy idea but it just might work, my inner, evil-genius, Bond-villain brain spoke to me.

I slid over to Iggy Barnes' locker. After checking to be sure the big bully wasn't anywhere in sight, I pulled out that orange and white shirt and stuffed it down deep into Iggy's backpack underneath some books, some snacks, and God knows what else. I looked around. Nobody had seen me. What Iggy would think on finding an orphaned shirt in his pack, I didn't know and didn't care. My hands were clean. I walked away.

CHAPTER 19 —

We walk half a mile down the road to a roadhouse, the kind of dark, scary bar your parents warned you against, a place any sane person would drive right past if they had an operating vehicle of any kind.

We walk right in.

I have some theories about bars, which have evolved over the years—the theories, not the bars. I used to think certain bars attract certain clientele, but now I think there's something about the bars themselves that fundamentally change the patrons. This one, for instance, off the main highway, a little ways from town, somewhere in Indiana, isn't particularly busy, but it's preternaturally quiet. The kind of drunks in there are getting more sullen with each drink, and angrier, and uglier, and more slumped over.

There are bars filled with laughter and music and dancing and jokes and joy—this isn't one of them. Is it Nature or is it Nurture? Did these people come in expecting a good time and were instead beaten down by the oppressive atmosphere of the place? Or did they bring that themselves, demanding the establishment and the others in attendance cater to their despondency?

It's hard to tell with this place. There's a pool table and a dart-board and a jukebox for entertainment but nobody looks like they're enjoying themselves. Despite the cold stares and threatening atmosphere, Gary walks right up to the bar and takes a stool. Ian and I follow, more reluctantly, spinning as we walk, keeping an eye out for trouble, like a couple of gunslingers. We sit.

I know I saw this scene in a movie once. *Easy Rider*. Except we're hardly hippies (well, maybe Gary is) and we're in our mid-fifties age-wise, and we're not the ones with motorcycles, *they* are. But then again, we're strangers from out of town—from New Jersey, for crying out loud. East Coasters. Liberal Elites. I have to laugh.

"What do you want?" the bartender asks, all Midwestern friendliness left outside apparently.

"Glass of beer," I say.

"Do you serve food?" Gary asks.

"I can make you cheeseburgers or I can make you eggs. Comes with mashed potatoes and gravy."

Gary hesitates, looking around as if he can't decide, or maybe he's thinking maybe he shouldn't eat anything here, not without a complete inspection from the Health Department including all the appropriate swab samples sent off for testing. Or maybe he's gonna inquire if the eggs are from "free-range" chickens, organically fed—

The bartender, who I now notice has only one working eye, shoots that orb over to Ian, who is also reticent to order anything.

"Gimme me a cheeseburger," I tell the man, just to let him and everyone else in the room know I'm a decisive person who knows what he wants. "And the potatoes and gravy."

"Comes with," the proprietor explains like I'm some kind of mental defective or something.

"I heard you," I answer, giving him my best smile—

"What about you girls?" the bartender asks the others.

"I'll have eggs, scrambled," Ian says. "And the potatoes and gravy."

"I'll take the same, but hold the gravy," Gary says.

"Comin' right up," the man says in the least hospitable way you can say that before he retreats through a swinging door to the kitchen. It's not clear if anyone's back there—maybe this guy does all the cooking himself.

"The jerk forgot my beer," I complain.

"Yeah, I want one, too," Gary says.

"I want one three," Ian chimes in.

A customer, a short, stocky guy with an orange ski-cap slips around behind the bar like he owns the place and starts drawing beers.

"Better not call Patch a jerk to his face," the guy advises. His arms are huge and so is his neck. He's young, maybe not even drinking age. He's trouble, that's for sure, and I make a "note to self" to take him out first thing when the fight starts, which I'm sure it will. He draws our three beers quickly, with a couple glances to the back room, but then he doesn't stop there, drawing more beers from the tap and slipping them down the bar to several of his friends, who grab them and back away in a hurry—

"Patch" returns. He notices we're sipping beers.

"They went behind the bar and took 'em themselves," one of the pool-players tells the bartender.

"No, we didn't," Ian states calmly and politely.

"You callin' me a liar?" The pool-player calls back, standing up from the table, gripping his cue, preparing to use it.

Meanwhile, orange-cap sneaks around to my left. I swivel and tense my right arm, gauging the distance, readying the ol' haymaker.

"Is that a Rolex?" he suddenly gushes, moving right up to my left hand.

"It is," I state.

"A *real* one?" the kid wants to know.

"It is," I tell him, though it's questionable. I'm not sure myself, but I know enough not to get it officially appraised. How I came by it is a long story I don't feel like sharing with this orange-headed punk right then.

"You boys don't know who we are, do you?" Ian announces to the room, sensing I'm in no shape for another knock-down drag-out—

"Yeah, who the fuck are you?" someone calls.

"They have no idea, do they?" Ian elbows me with a laugh. "Not a clue. Or where we're from."

"So, where the fuck are you from?" somebody else wants to know.

"New Jersey," Gary answers proudly.

"Our deepest fucking condolences," a wag smirks.

"You ever watch *The Sopranos*?" Ian challenges.

Shaking heads all around.

"*Goodfellas*? *The Godfather*?"

"I saw that," someone in the back speaks up. "*Godfather II* was even better—"

"Fuck no!" somebody wants to argue.

"Well, this gentleman here," Ian says, putting his hand on my shoulder, "just happens to be Scotty 'The Fist' Carollo."

A hushed silence descends over the room.

"Big deal."

"I still say we bust his ass—"

Murmuring takes over, which sounds like "bourbon Bromo-Seltzer" repeated over and over, and I can see whatever Ian's trying to pull isn't going to work with this crowd no matter how many cultural references we have in common.

"Gentlemen, gentlemen!" Ian calls out as the mob shuffles forward. "What about *Breaking Bad*?"

They hesitate. I wouldn't have pegged them as an AMC cable crowd but there it was.

"You know how they were going to build a giant underground drug lab?" Ian says.

"Hey, spoiler alert!" someone calls out, which gets a big laugh.

"Well, what if I were to tell you we were here to scout a location out in the middle of nowhere to do just that, like in the show," Ian says. "Ten thousand square feet of space, underground, with jobs for a hundred men and women, maybe a thousand or more good-paying positions once we get up and running. With all sorts of spillover spending—gas stations, mortuaries, souvenir shops, even this establishment right here could benefit enormously from the influx of cash and personnel and human traffic."

The locals are impressed, the poor slobs.

Ian pauses, giving their tiny brains a chance to digest what he's saying. Our food comes. More beers are poured. Ian tries the mashed potatoes, seems surprised by the taste, and manages not to choke.

"This is—" He swallows. "—very good," he manages.

Okay, so maybe they don't completely buy the idea we're a bunch of Mafioso types who've come to bring prosperity to their fucked-up little town—nobody's that stupid. But on the other hand, if even a tenth of what Ian says is true, nobody wants to be the one to question it and ruin it for their families, friends and neighbors, just in case it *is* true. It's an emperor has no clothes situation, and there's no pesky kid in that bar that night to point it out—

Except for orange-cap, who accosts us in the parking lot with a gun in his hand.

"Gimme the Rolex," he demands.

"You don't want to do this, son," I tell the punk, surprising myself—I sound like my Old Man. I never called anyone "son," even my own boys.

"I don't, do I?" the orange-capped kid hisses.

"No, you don't," Ian interrupts, stepping in front of me, prepared to take the bullet. "Let me tell you about that Rolex," he says, speaking urgently. "It's stolen. And during the robbery a man was killed. A police officer. War hero. If that Rolex was traced to you, you'd get the death penalty if the cops didn't kill you first."

The kid looks at me. My sincere silence convinces him. He turns and walks away, gun hanging harmlessly at his side.

"Fuck you," he says. "Fuck all of you."

CHAPTER 20 —

I learned to fight like most boys, from watching old Westerns on TV. Of course, that was all pure fiction, and in a real fight, things generally go much differently. Especially when it comes to the haymaker. In the movies, they'd swing one after another, connecting with jaw every time, and then the last poor sap who got hit would jump up and lay one on the other guy, who'd take it on the chin, look dazed for a second, then swing back. In real life, I only needed to swing that fist once. I was big and I was strong, but I wasn't the biggest or the strongest, but with that haymaker, it was "lights out." So, I practiced that swing. Why make it a big, long, drawn-out fight when you can end it with one punch? That's what I was practicing that night with the mailboxes.

We had a couple friends—brothers—twins—I won't give their names. Irish, a little older than us by a couple years. Crazy, even more than us. They were supposed to be watching their parents house for the weekend. They were tough guys, way more tough than us, but for some reason we got along, even with Gary and Ian along. We showed up with a gallon of white wine we'd stolen from somewhere. The twins had a bunch of beer and wine, so we did what we always did, which was to get totally fucked up and then keep on drinking and smoking.

We walked home, I recall, because we were too wasted to stay on our bikes.

So, here's the setup. Nowa-days, most mailboxes are mounted up right next to the houses where the occupant can step out to the front porch and the mail is right there. Or some places have a slot in the front door, and you can pick up your mail without ever going outside. All very convenient for the postal customer, but hell on the mailman who has to walk up each and every walkway and driveway. But back then the area was still being suburbanized and the boxes were all out next to the street on wooden posts so the mailman could walk or drive right down the row without any hassle. Designed for a postman on horseback, really.

And also perfect for my purpose, which was to perfect my haymaker. I walked down the street, hitting one after another—BOOM!—knocking those mailboxes clean off the posts or cracking the posts themselves, breaking them off, damaging every single mailbox. All the while Ian and Gary and Jess kept a running tab:

"Ten...eleven...twelve!"

A chant really, which got all the dogs on the street barking and raising a clamor. Too much noise for midnight in a quiet town like Oakburgh. Houselights came on, then porch lights, but we were too drunk to notice. Then came the siren.

"Run!" Jess yelled and we all ran down the street in a bunch, which wasn't the best strategy.

"Split up!" Ian shouted.

We scattered. I went down a county road, unpaved and dark—no streetlights.

A police prowler came around the corner ahead of me. There was no place to hide and no place to run to, but the night was dark and so were the clothes I wore, so I flopped down on the thick grass of somebody's front yard and stayed very still, which was easy after all the wine and beer and dope. But my breath sounded like a tornado roaring out from me, so I held it in, hoping the cop wouldn't see or hear me. If he used his spotlight, I was toast...

But he didn't use his light, perhaps out of politeness to the people sleeping in their warm, friendly houses in their quiet neighborhood. After the car passed and I was sure the cop wasn't coming back (the kind of trick those cops like to pull), I stood up and started walking. A couple more cars came down the road—it was suddenly Times Square there—so I dropped prone on the ground again each time and wasn't spotted. At the corner, a patrol car came around and caught me in its lights before I had a chance to pull the stunt again. I tried to walk casually tough to do on purpose. I'm sure I looked guilty as hell.

The car slowed and I prepared to pull my best "evening officer" act, like I was just another Joe Citizen walking around after midnight (which never happened in Oakburgh). To my dismay, the cruiser stopped, and a cop jumped out. To my further dismay, it wasn't Officer Hank

Polensky, who wouldn't have made such a big deal out of a bunch of mailboxes, I'm pretty sure.

"Hold it right there!" the cop ordered like I was Machine Gun Kelly or something.

"Evening, officer," I called to him. "Nice night for a stroll."

Which was when I noticed Gary in the back seat of the patrol car, head bent in despair and sitting in an awkward position with his hands behind his back, indicating to anyone looking at him that he was handcuffed.

"Oh, thank God!" I cried out. "You found him! My aunt was so worried!" I skipped over to the police car and tried to open the door. It was locked. "Please, " I said to the cop, "open the door. My cousin Jimmy. He ran away. He's a retard, see—he can't be out alone. He'll get lost. I've been out looking for him. Let him go so I can get him home." I could see the policeman wasn't buying it. I doubled down: "I know, I know—I shouldn't have said 'retard.' You're not supposed to say that anymore. It's 'mentally deficient' or some shit. Sorry, I shouldn't have said 'shit,' either. Brain-fucked, really dumb as a doornail, this guy. Hey there, buddy, don't worry. This nice officer's gonna let you go home."

"Thought you said you were out for a stroll," the policeman snickered.

"Out for a stroll looking for my stupid cousin Johnny."

"Seems bright enough to me," the policeman replied, casually stepping around the car in my direction. "What did you say his name was?"

I couldn't remember what I'd said. Johnny or Jimmy or something.

"Mind if I take a look at those knuckles of yours?" the cop asked, reaching for his flashlight.

I ran!

The cop chased me, but I was younger and faster.

"Stop or I'll shoot!" he shouted.

"No, you won't!" I shouted back. He didn't. I knew he wouldn't. To be brutally honest, he was a white cop in a white town in middle-class New Jersey and I was a white teenager. He wasn't going to shoot me in the back, even in the 1980s.

I made it to the woods behind the houses—*my* territory, my safe place. Back then the woods connected all around to the back of my house a mile or so away. I was home free, for the moment, at least. Not so good for Gary, but I figured he wouldn't rat us out, no matter how much pressure they put him under. They'd call his two dads and they'd both have to come down to the station and there'd be a harsh lecture about hanging around with the wrong people (me) but that would be it, I figured.

I made it home, snuck into the house and passed out on my bed. An hour or so later, in the middle of the night, there was a knock on my door.

"Scotty, get up and get dressed and come to the kitchen," I heard my dad order and by the tone of his voice I knew it was gonna be bad.

I walked into the kitchen and there were my parents and the police officer who chased me. The cop was so angry if my dad wasn't there, he would've kicked my ever-lovin' ass, or *shot* me in the ass, small suburban town or not, white or black, an equal opportunity butt-massacre. The Old Man wasn't too far behind. I found out later that when the cop got back in the prowler and sped around to chase me, he'd run over a cat and killed it, and apparently this cop was a strong animal lover. It didn't help that he was also a born-again Christian, God help us all. And oh yeah, his sister was "developmentally disabled." So how was I supposed to know that? Fuggedaboutit.

My main mantra in those days was "deny deny deny," which I did until the policeman got a good look at my knuckles, which were scarred and bruised and discolored from the manly art of mailbox punching.

Gary sang like a canary and gave us all up.

Fortunately, we didn't get sent to Juve, just forty hours of community service.

Gary was banned from the group. We vowed never to forgive him or to speak to him again.

CHAPTER 21 —

With nothing else to do until the Argo gets fixed—"In a day or two," the guy says—we hang around town. It's a nice enough place, a railroad stop, a place for farmers to bring their goods and buy the tools and seed they need for the next season, but what do I know? I'm a farmer all of a sudden?

Most of the shops have turned into "crafts" emporiums for people coming in off the highway. It's all handmade stuff and some antiques and everybody's got a website, so most of their business comes that way, I figure. Nobody's making a killing, I'm pretty sure. We go eat breakfast at the café along with everyone else in town, it seems. Immediately we get the idea that word has spread about the "gangsters in town" from the night before. A few customers jump up and leave to stay out of the line of fire, but most just gawk at us. We wave back and call "good morning" to them, which makes a few more make a run for it.

The waitress is so nervous, I'm afraid she's gonna drop dead before she gets our orders down on the quivering notepad in front of her. At that point, the tow-truck kid from the day before rushes in and tells us the Argo will be ready in twenty-four hours, even though they need to drive to the next town over to pick up some parts on a rush basis.

"They're in a hurry to get rid of us," I remark to Ian and Gary after the young man leaves.

"No, they're scared of us," Gary says. "You especially," he adds, pointing at me. "They don't want to get you pissed—no telling what you'll do."

"Getouddahere," I reply.

"What they really want is the money," Ian whispers.

"The money?" I ask.

"The money from the giant underground drug lab they think we're going to build," Ian says.

"Getouddahere," I repeat. "Nobody believes that crap."

"They believe it because they want to believe it," Ian says. "They're tired of knitting oven-mitts and tea-cozies. They're looking for some action."

Ian's right, of course; it's obvious by the way we're treated. Ian and Gary milk it for the rest of the day, pretending to be interested in property values, empty lots, railroad connections, "tonnage," all the while talking into their phones to "headquarters," "the boss," and other made-up connections. I refuse to go along with this bullshit, even though I'm the actual expert at it, having worked in the warehouse/transportation sector my entire working life.

"Cut it out," I finally tell them, putting my foot down. "This is a dangerous game you're playing."

"Jeez, Dad, can't we have any fun?" Gary answers.

"In the first place, did it ever occur to you there might be law enforcement around somewhere and if everybody else thinks we're here to start up a major drug operation, maybe they'll hear about it, too?"

Gary and Ian don't have anything to say to that.

"And did you think there might *already* be a drug distribution operation of some sort here, and those people might not appreciate us honing in?"

Gary and Ian shuffle their feet. They know I'm right. I take the Rolex out of my pocket (where I'm keeping it for now) and check the time.

"Just a few more hours of daylight," I say. "I suggest we go back to the motel, lay low and see if they got cable."

Ian and Gary agree. I put the watch back in my pocket.

"By the way, if it's any of your business, which it ain't," I tell them, "I didn't steal this watch and I don't think it's fake. But I'll never know, 'cause I won't ever have it appraised, just in case."

"So maybe my story was true," Ian gloats.

"No, that was bullshit," I tell him.

CHAPTER 22 —

I was riding my bike over to Ian's one Saturday when I heard shouting from the next street over. The voices sounded familiar. I went to see what was up. In the little downtown area, there was an empty lot—municipal parking—and in the middle of it Officer Hank Polensky faced off with Iggy Barnes. I hit the brakes on my bike and hung back.

Iggy wore my orange and white striped T-shirt!

And Officer Hank was trying to arrest him.

"I don't know what you're talking about, dude!" Iggy squawked. "What apples? I don't even like apples. I didn't steal no apples. Who steals apples?"

"I'm arresting you."

"For what?"

"Throwing apples."

"Who does that?"

"You did. And the charge is assault on a police officer," the cop declared.

"Now wait a minute—"

"We got you dead to rights. You're wearing the same shirt—"

"I found this shirt—"

"You're just lucky nobody got hurt—"

"You're saying throwing apples is a crime?"

"If you throw 'em at a police officer, it is," Officer Hank insisted. "Now put your hands on the hood of the patrol car."

I suppose it was funny. I should have laughed. It was the kind of prank we used to pull in those days, but at the time I felt sort of sorry for Iggy, no matter how many kids he'd terrorized.

I never told the other guys about that day. I never said a word about Iggy or the shirt or

this encounter with Officer Hank, which was prior to the incident that got Hank killed. To Jess and Ian and Gary that night had all been a random, absurd tragedy, which it was, but not exactly as it appeared to be, or how they saw it.

CHAPTER 23 —

"Bingo!" Ian declares from the back seat. "I got it!"

Gary and I give each other a look. We're back on the road, almost out of Indiana, nearing Illinois. The Argo, still a little dinged body-wise (which kills me), is driving fine.

"Got what?" I ask, playing along, 'cause I really don't care.

"I got a refund on the gas we never put in."

"That was two days ago," I remark.

"Hey, it's still money," Ian notes.

I'm not going to argue, and neither is Gary. We exchange another look.

"I'm so happy for you," I tell Ian.

CHAPTER 24 —

We were out in the woods, drinking as usual, on a Friday night. Suddenly Ian looked up and stared into the darkness in the direction of town.

"Well, looky here," Ian said.

We could tell it was Gary just by the way he walked, which was kind of a rising and falling gait, as if his feet had a mind of their own, independent of Gary's brain. It had been three or four months since the night of the crashing mailboxes, and none of us had spoken to him since.

Gary carried a gallon jug of wine. He offered it to Ian first.

"No cups?" Ian complained. "How we supposed to drink this shit?"

"Like moonshine, bro," I said, wrestling the bottle from him, unscrewing the cap. I nested the thing in the crook of my arm, hoisted it up, turned my head and drank greedily from the lip. Of course I didn't know shit about moonshine; this was something I'd picked up from *The Beverly Hillbillies*, most likely. We passed the bottle around and it wasn't bad wine—not too sweet like a lot of the cheap stuff.

Nobody said a word about the mailboxes or Gary ratting us out or the forty hours of community service we'd all been sentenced to, picking up trash along the roads and highways, and repairing mailboxes, all without exchanging a word with Gary.

Now it was as if we'd all forgotten it, erased from memory like in *Men in Black* (spoiler alert).

CHAPTER 25 —

We cross the Mississippi in St. Louis, driving across the Stan Musial Veterans Memorial Bridge, known locally as the "Stan Span." It chokes me up a little, crossing from the East (the Old World) to the West, Parts Unknown. I'm not a sentimental guy, but it occurs to me that while I might be driving back the other way in the near future, Jess wouldn't. Not ever. I spell Mississippi a couple times in my mind, something I started doing in the third grade. I used to be able to spell hippopotamus, too, but those days are long-gone—too many knocks on the head, too many beers, too much dope.

I see Ian and Gary give each other a look. Amused, they are.

"What?" I ask.

"You're not going to spell it?" Gary asks.

"You can't wait to spell it," Ian needles.

"Itching to," Gary piles on.

"Cut it out," I protest. There's no way I'll give them the satisfaction.

Gary curls up in his seat and closes his eyes.

"Wake me if you see a hippopotamus."

CHAPTER 26 —

We all graduated from high school together, even me. I always knew I was smart enough, but no one (including me) guessed I could apply myself to that extent. The next week I had a union job at a giant warehouse—a job the Old Man got me. I met Angie a year later, through work—she was involved in shipping relief supplies to Eastern Europe if I remember right, after the fall of the Berlin Wall and the Iron Curtain.

I'm doing that same job, basically, that I started out at, though fifty times the scale, and I'm in charge of it all. "Trucks in, trucks out" pretty much sums it up. Goods come in, goods go out, and I need to make sure that happens smoothly or as close to smoothly as I can make it. I'm not as rigid as Ian and not as disorganized as Gary.

We have a nice house—the basic three bedroom, nicely landscaped, just to brag a little. (I do most of the yard work myself, and not entirely because I'm cheap.)

Angie's still a do-gooder, and like me, she's moved up in rank. She no longer has to concern herself with every can of beans or bag of rice, but instead "consults" in the comfort of our own home, coming up with schemes to relieve other do-gooders of their money so the organizations she works for can buy, ship and distribute the stuff and try to keep people alive all over the world. It's a losing battle, but I don't tell her that. She knows it, too, I'm pretty sure, but she does it anyway and I love her for it.

I've lived my life for her and haven't regretted a single moment. And for the kids, of course. We have two sons, Daniel and Tyler, both college grads. Daniel's the older of the two, almost thirty now. He's smart like his mother, and just got his PhD in Medieval Studies. He's a teacher, and he'll be happy with that, which I don't understand one bit. He's got a lot of Ian in him, but also some Jess. Daniel's got a daughter of his own, Amy, just five years old now, and they go camping whenever they can up in Massachusetts, where they live. Angie and I go visit when we can, and they come down for Christmas and Easter and Thanksgiving.

Tyler's our younger son. He's more like me, a big kid, who gravitated to sports early on. He played high school football and basketball and wrestling and track and all that. He's a hot head like me, I gotta admit, and used to get in a bunch of fights. Nothing like us of course—the next generation didn't come close to the freedom and independence we had—or the scars. We were like a wild, untamed tribe of nomads; Daniel and Tyler were kept safe, organized, always accompanied by adults, one structured activity after another. I know there are reasons for it—guns and knives and craziness we didn't face when we were kids, or maybe we were just too stupid to recognize the dangers.

Tyler now coaches high school football and swimming and teaches gym in a suburban school outside of Philly. He isn't married yet, but there's always a girlfriend around, though never the same one twice in a row, we've noticed. But there's still hope.

If Daniel's an Ian type, with a little Jess thrown in, Tyler's me (ruggedly handsome), with some Gary in there, 'cause despite all Tyler's angry energy there's a core of kindness and understanding below the surface. Again, that's Angie's doing, no doubt.

I'm thinking about them all and wondering what they're doing at that precise moment as I drive west into the sun. I remind myself to stop early enough to call Angie and say goodnight. I wonder where the time zone changes to Central Time. I could ask the phone, of course—it probably does it automatically anyway—*but it's easier just to ask Ian,* I chuckle to myself.

I think about the two years I spent in the Army. I enlisted right after 9/11. Angie didn't squawk about it, though she could have. At the least she was left alone to take care of a one-year-old baby; at worst I could've gotten myself blown up on some roadside in Afghanistan. Besides, I was thirty-one years of age and the cutoff for the Army was thirty-five; nobody expected me to enlist. As it turns out, what the army needed most was a good quartermaster, a warehouse man, trucks in and out,

Humvees in and out, planes and boats, logistics. My name was all over that; I was their man, all safely behind the battle-lines—Fort Dix, Fort Stewart, Fort Riley, Fort Meade. I saw more mess halls, more warehouses, and more landing fields than any man alive, but I never saw combat, and never left the confines of the United States.

Gary stirs and wakens in the passenger's seat next to me. I put my finger to my lips and nod my head to the back, where Ian is now sleeping. Gary understands; he doesn't speak.

"You did the right thing, you know," I whispered to Gary. He looks at me, then out the window. There are a hundred "right things" I could be talking about, but I can see he knows exactly which one I'm referring to. I also notice that a heavy weight seems to have been lifted from his shoulders. "US code 1705, destruction of a mailbox,"

I go on in a low voice. "Federal crime. Three years in prison."

"We were juveniles," Gary shrugs. "They probably wouldn't have tried us as adults."

"But they could have," I assure him. "You saved us. You did good."

Gary nods a thank you. We drive on into the dimming light. I glance back in the rear-view mirror. Ian's awake, eyes open and staring out into the darkness. I can't tell if he heard our conversation or not.

CHAPTER 27 —

Jess got out of town immediately after graduation. It might have even been the same day. One day he was there, the next he was gone. We stood at his front door, bewildered.

"He went where?" I asked his mother again, who was obviously distraught.

"The note didn't say, exactly. The West, the Rocky Mountains, the Grand Tetons. He mentioned them all."

I was overcome with the misery of it all. I suddenly saw Jess's mother in an entirely new light. Here she was, alone, abandoned again. All those times when Jess's dad came home from deployment—how she must have felt with her husband and Jess going out camping, leaving her in the house. Now it would be a permanent abandonment. She could see that, and so could I, even as a stupid-ass high-school graduate. I wanted to hold Mrs. Freeman and stroke her hair and tell her it'd be okay, and I'd be there always for her. And then, in my mind, we'd screw.

"It's all he ever wanted to do," Mrs. Freeman lamented. "Like he was Daniel Boone or something."

"Yeah, he was nuts that way," Ian chimed in, no doubt trying to make Jess's mom feel better, failing miserably at it.

My anger at Jess for leaving his mother that way lasts to this day. He did send her a postcard a month later, letting her know he was okay, giving her a post office address. He sent one to Ian, too, which we passed around at our camp one night in the woods behind my house. It said he was learning to ski and washing dishes at a resort northwest of Denver, high in the Rockies.

"He's gonna get so much pussy," Gary noted.

"Yeah," Ian and I agreed.

A month later Gary was gone, too, all the way to the Shoreline Amphitheatre on the outskirts of San Francisco, to catch the Dead tour. He sent pictures and t-shirts, the last we heard from him for awhile.

Ian went to Rutgers. I stayed in Oakburgh.

"We're not college people," the Old Man always said.

Me, Ian, Jess and Gary lost touch off and on over time, sometimes for years but amazingly, we never *really* drifted apart, even with Jess two-thirds of the country away, and Gary with all his travels. Thanks to the internet for that, and cellphones. It was easy to keep up.

CHAPTER 28 —

So, I’m driving (I've decided I'll do all the driving the whole way) when suddenly Gary pulls a harmonica out of his pocket like we're in a Kris Kristofferson song or something. He plays "Red River Valley" on it and now we're in more of a John Ford Western. He plays it slow and sad, with a ton of vibrato. I glance in the rearview mirror. Me and Ian give each other a look, but we don't say anything snide or snarky, though we've got big grins on our faces, and we could burst out laughing at any moment at how hokey it all is. Gary ends the song on a long, wavering note, milking it. I start to say something, but Gary doesn't stop playing long enough, instead launching into a rendition of "Streets of Laredo," making it twice as cornball as the first song.

I've known Gary for fifty years and never knew he played the harmonica, or any other instrument for that matter, or that he even had an interest or talent for anything musical. He was looney-tunes about The Grateful Dead, following them to Hell and back, and maybe I pictured him banging on a tambourine and stomping around in a circle like an Indian chief's trusted Holy Man, but not this.

"What the fuck?" I say simply.

Gary grins sheepishly.

"How long have you been playing the harmonica?" Ian asks from the back seat.

Gary blushes, an odd thing for a man his age.

"Awhile," he answers vaguely.

"News to me," I say. "You keeping it a big secret?"

"I knew you'd just bust my balls about it," Gary sighs.

"Hey, fuggedaboutit," I declare. "A guy wants to play the harmonica, what do I care? What business is it of mine if a guy wants to do that...or play the accordion or the bagpipes or the pan-flute, no matter how annoying to everyone around him."

"That's big of you," Gary says with a smile. I can see he would've been disappointed if we *hadn't* busted his balls.

"We just didn't know," Ian chimes in from the back.

"There's lots of things you don't know about me," Gary answers, but not all bragging and mysterioso the way I'd say it, but genuine, heartfelt.

"Oh yeah, you're a man of mystery," I can't help saying.

"Jerry Garcia gave this to me," Gary says, ignoring the sarcasm, holding up the harmonica.

"Get out," I play along, pretending to be impressed. Actually, I am.

"He said he didn't get much chance to play it anymore."

"Probably 'cause he's *dead*," Ian remarks behind us.

I stifle a laugh. Gary lets it slide.

"This was before he died, of course. He said he had too many harmonicas and didn't have time to play this one so much."

We all think about that.

"Let me get this straight—he gave you a *used* harmonica?"

"Yeah."

"That he'd put his mouth on and spit in and slobbered all over?" I press.

"Yeah, he'd played it. But it was pretty dry—"

"Yuck."

In the back seat, Ian's laughing and gripping his sides.

"It wasn't like that."

"Your good friend Jerry Garcia dissed you like that?"

"He wasn't my good friend."

It gets quiet again. Maybe I've gone too far.

"I guess not," I say, unable to resist one last dig.

"I only met him a few times, actually," Gary confesses. "He nodded to me whenever he saw me, though. I was a familiar face, but he didn't know me from Adam. A lot of people followed the band around. I wasn't the only one."

All is silence again. To say we are embarrassed for Gary is an understatement. To say we understand the pain he feels at this moment would be a lie. Nevertheless, the world gets a little heavier on our shoulders—*that* we know.

"Play something else," I tell Gary.

CHAPTER 29 —

To everyone's relief, Officer Hank Polensky died three weeks after Iggy hit him with the iron bar. He didn't linger and he didn't suffer and neither did his wife or any other family members, if he had any, but that didn't make our pact any less valid, according to Jess. We kept going around to see Mrs. Polensky a few times a week even after her husband was dead—it seemed too cruel not to. We helped around the house as much as we could, but frankly we weren't good at housekeeping, and probably did more harm than good. She thanked us and told us how nice we were to keep her company, but she said it so many times it got to be embarrassing, and we ended up not going around there anymore. Then one day there was a For Sale sign on the lawn in front, and Teresa Polensky was gone.

Iggy pled guilty to assault, or aggravated assault, or something like that. The big, ugly sap had just turned eighteen, so he was treated as an adult. He got seven years in Rahway. Everyone said he was lucky since it was a law enforcement officer he struck and killed, but seven years hard time didn't sound like luck to me. The TV and the papers played up what a hero Polensky was and what a warm, caring human being he was, and how he'd be missed terribly in "the community." They write these things up far in advance and just plug in the names when the time comes. As for Oakburgh being a "community," well, maybe it was in some weird way, but I didn't see it that way—more of collection of unconnected families.

Jerry Garcia died August 9, 1995. Gary showed up in Oakburgh a month later and moved back in with his parents, his Dead days over. In some ways it was perfect—

he made it just in time for my wedding to Angie, which was a giant affair, a huge embarrassment in fact, because of its size, but that was all the Old Man's doing, a way to show off to all his cronies and tell them what a deal he got on the cake and the caterer and the band, all because he "knew some people." Ian and Gary were there, and I wish Jess had made it, but according to his email it was "prime rafting season," and he was too busy taking tourists down the Snake River or the Green River or some river or another.

Bastard.

We should've made a pact about *that*—going to each other's weddings.

Ian, always a copy-cat, got married a year later to a gorgeous girl he met at Rutgers. I don't remember her name. For awhile they seemed happy enough, but then they moved back to Oakburgh and bought a house close to Ian's parents, which any idiot could see was a huge mistake. Add to that, she was an Ohio girl, homesick for the cows, I suppose, and wanted to move back there. Her major was Supply Chain Management of all things, which made me laugh. *College for that?* It's what I did every day, of course, and she wanted to talk to me about it—pick my brain, so to speak—but I wouldn't have it. Not that I was afraid of giving away trade secrets, it's just I didn't think it was a good idea and would only get me in trouble with Ian one way or another (she was that gorgeous).

When she asked me for a job at my warehouse, I turned her down flat, even though I really wasn't in charge of hiring or firing people (that would come later). She moved back to Ohio soon after that, without Ian, and that was the end of their marriage. To her credit, she never told Ian I had turned her down. He would definitely have mentioned it. So maybe their divorce was my fault. I don't know. Maybe everything's my fault.

Ian sold his house and moved back in with his parents "to take care of them," which was wildly inaccurate since they immediately took off traveling the world like they'd always planned. Ian stuck to business, a variety of schemes which brought untold millions, I think, though Ian never bragged about it or bought fancy cars or a yacht or houses on the Riviera. His parents did all that, though.

My parents moved to Florida. They live in one of those "villages" made up of house trailers, but don't you dare call them "house trailers." "Manufactured Homes" is the preferred term. To be fair, they're just as large and nice as any other housing, and the fact each house has a license plate and a set of wheels somewhere under it is really only a legal nicety, apparently. Angie and I go down and visit once or twice a year for a few days each time. The Old Man is still wheeling and dealing, trading goods out of the "day room" behind the carport, anxious to let everybody know he deals only in questionable merchandise, wink wink, that "fell off the back of a truck," which for some reason seems to increase the value in everyone's mind. My older sister, Carolyn, got married and had a couple of kids, who are now out of college and on their own. Carolyn married a real estate guy who made a killing in all the housing booms and busts of the last thirty years. They live north of San Diego next to the sea and their only worry is the place will fall into the ocean at some point or another, or burn to the ground, or shake to rubble, or they'll be killed in a home-invasion robbery, or a drive-by shooting, or a road-rage incident. But what are you gonna do?

My little brother is also married with two kids. He lives a little closer to me—Chicago, actually—and I considered going that way on the drive to Denver, but Ian and Gary vetoed the idea.

"Too far out of the way," they said, "and too much bad weather," but I suspect there were other reasons. Neither of them has brothers or sisters. Both of them are only children. The same with Jess, and I realized I was the only one of us with siblings. Which would explain a lot, I guess, if I ever wanted to think about it.

Angie and I considered having another kid, maybe two, but we never really decided yes or no. Eventually time slipped away, and we ended up not having any more. If either of us regrets it, we don't say. There's a lot we don't say, but that doesn't make us any less happy or any less in love.

Gary's two fathers moved to San Franscisco and are active in the gay rights movement, which is about right—they always seemed to be about twenty-five years behind times.

Jess's mother moved to Texas, and it wasn't clear whether Jess's Marine Corps father went with her or not. We never saw them again, though Jess came back to New Jersey a few times over the decades, usually staying at Ian's house, not because they were best buds, but because Ian had the most space.

CHAPTER 30 —

"Ladies and germs," I announce. "If you look out to your right, on the horizon, you can see Topeka, Kansas, and the capitol dome."

There it was, a bright, white sphere, glowing in the sun.

"Big deal," Ian says. "They all look the same."

After that, it's ten or twelve hours of driving—I lose track—a straight shot to Denver, a couple stops on the way to piss and refuel and eat crappy food. The "empty quarter" I remember seeing on an old map once.

Denver isn't what I expected. I don't know what I expect, actually. Rising out of the Earth like the Emerald City of Oz? It's more of a gradual climb from the Kansas border, the air becoming thinner and colder, the vehicle feeling the grade, too. It sneaks up on you, the crisp beauty of it all, and then you're in one more urban landscape, but it's different, cleaner and brighter, the West, with endless possibilities. For someone. Maybe not Jess. Maybe not us. Maybe it's just the lack of oxygen talking.

We check into a pretty good hotel in downtown Denver—not the best but also not the most expensive. Ian's research says it's a good deal, so me and Gary go along. What do I care? It's late and I want to call Angie back home where it's even two hours later.

"I'll get something to eat from room service and see you bright and early tomorrow," I tell Ian and Gary.

"Eight o'clock?" Ian suggests. "That's when visiting hours—"

"That's good," I interrupted, grabbing my bag and sprinting for the elevator. I don't need reminding of why we're here.

As I ride up to my room, I wonder if I've made a mistake letting Ian and Gary loose on the unsuspecting city of Denver. It's early in the evening; who knows what kind of trouble they could get into with this much time on their hands? Without me to watch over them and protect them. I check—the car-keys are safely in my pocket.

Fuggedaboutit, I tell myself. I'm not their babysitter. Maybe there'd been a time in junior high and high school when I took on that role, no matter how ridiculous. *Maybe that's why you never had any more kids,* it occurs to me. You had Jess and Ian and Gary to look after all those years.

But that time's over, motherfucker, I tell myself. *Right here and right now in this smelly old elevator*, I vow, *that time's over.*

We meet in the hotel's café at eight the next morning. To my surprise, Ian and Gary are on time, and seem wide-awake, and there are no visible scars. Still, I refrain from asking what they'd done the night before.

While we drive to the hospital, Gary lights up a bowl-full of pot and smokes it down, offering none of it to me and Ian (who's in the back checking on Colorado's dope laws on his phone).

The hospital is like every other hospital—bright and clean and antiseptic smelling, just barely covering a hundred other unpleasant odors. There's no problem getting in to see Jess, and I can't help contrasting this with sneaking in to see Officer Hank all those years before. We're middle-aged, respectable looking now, not the juvenile delinquents we were before. I resent it and actually feel like breaking something, or stealing something, or sexually harassing the nurses. Within minutes we're standing in a private intensive care room looking down at the lifeless body of Jessup Freeman, just like we'd stared down at Officer Hank Polensky. Jess is hooked up to all kinds of machinery and there are bags of liquid hanging from a hat-rack next to him—IV fluid, medications, I don't know—what am I, a doctor?

Dead meat, that's all we are, on the road to dust. Unprocessed compost. Pathetic, really. Why had we come all this way? I glance up at Ian, the picture of frozen anxiety. I see his mind creaking, coming up with ways to solve problems nobody ever had, imagining dangers at every turn, shaking with fear at the prospect.

"We gotta have a plan!" he used to say.

Fuck that, I tell myself. There's no plan here. Jess is going to die, the way Hank did earlier. Nothing we can do about it except make it happen faster.

I look over at Gary at the opposite end of the spectrum, already high as a kite this early in the morning, but not relaxed—frazzled and fried in his own way just as much as Ian.

I fart, as loud as I can make it.

"Jesus!" Gary declares but can't help himself laughing.

"Cut it out, you two," Ian admonishes.

"Okay, Mom," I shoot back, offering up another wild, wet one, smellier than the first.

"Jesus!" Gary repeats, covering his nose, pushing his way past Ian to escape.

"Cut it out," Ian tells me.

"Just breaking the tension," I shrug innocently.

"Breaking *something,*" Ian comments, succumbing to the fumes himself, charging out of the crowded space to the hall, leaving me alone with Jess.

Alone...

It's all I can do to stay standing. I'm alone with the guy. *Is this when I'm supposed to do it? Pull the plug?* There are so many plugs. *Which one? All of them?*

Would there be a violent reaction, or would Jess just drift off to a permanent sleep, peacefully, without drama? I wish I'd looked this up. I clearly wasn't prepared. Why hadn't Ian, Mr. Anal Retentive, figured this out?

I notice Jess has a beard half going—do people grow beards in a coma? How about after death? Or is that just fingernails? I make a mental note to look that up or get Ian to look it up. Mostly I'm a little shocked how "ordinary"

Jess looks, like any other middle-aged man. He was always the fit one, with a slim body, the picture of health, the mountain man. Now, not so much.

I get angry, the way I always get angry, filtered down from other emotions I can't deal with until all that's left is anger. Why had Jess put us in this position? Why had he insisted on the pact? Was he even thinking? There'd been all these botched executions lately—it wasn't easy to put a man to death, it turns out, not in any humane way.

"Fuck this shit," I declare. Now even my own farts—which I once didn't mind at all—smelled sour and nasty.

I catch my reflection in the windowed wall to the hallway. Bruised and battered, I'm as worked-over and hopeless as Gary, and as internally damaged as Ian. I'm no different than either one. I can move, sure, unlike Jess at this moment, but that's little consolation.

CHAPTER 31 —

"I'd just off myself," Jess declared. "If I was in that situation, I'd just kill myself. Put an end to it. I couldn't be a burden to my family and my friends that way."

"Hank doesn't have any friends," Ian remarked, maybe a joke, maybe just fact.

"Sure he has friends," Gary offered. "He must."

"*We* are his friends," Jess said.

"That's pretty sad," I remarked.

Everybody got real quiet then. We stared into the little fire we'd built—small so nobody would call the fire department, but hot.

The fires of Hell, I couldn't keep from thinking.

"We should help him out," Gary said. "That's what real friends would do."

"We aren't his friends," I stated for the record. "We're teenaged punks."

"Help him out how?" Ian asked, though you could see by the look on his face he knew exactly how.

"He means pull the plug," I stated, since nobody else was going to say it out loud.

We agreed to go back and see Hank again the next day and decide after that what to do. We'd look around, come up with a way to do it maybe.

"We're just going to look, okay?" I insisted sternly. They all stared at me like "who the fuck are you, our leader all of a sudden?"

"Just look," Jess agreed.

He was our leader. We would do what he said. I was the muscle all right, and Ian was the brains, but Jess was our leader. We would follow him anywhere. Together, we stood as one and put our hands out over the fire, forming a single mighty fist.

Yeah, we were pretty young...

CHAPTER 32 —

I step out into the hall, thinking it's typical of both Gary and Ian to drag me all this way, even make me drive, just to abandon me in the intensive care room alone with Jess. They stand down the hall in a little visitors and employees break area with some tables and chairs and vending machines, which they check in dead earnest despite the fact we've just come from eating a big hotel breakfast.

"What are you two ass-holes doing out here?" I hiss at them.

"Waiting for the air to clear," Ian shoots back. "Fuck it—I'm going to talk to him."

With that, Ian marches back to the room, me and Gary in pursuit.

"This place gives me the creeps," Ian tells Jess right off. "What the hell are you doing out here anyway, Jess?" There's no answer. "It's like a rodeo's gonna break out at any moment."

"And the food sucks—seriously, their signature dish is a cheese omelet," Gary jumps in.

"With little peppers in it," Ian says.

"La-de-dah," Gary says.

Jess doesn't laugh. Nobody laughs.

We stay for another hour or so, talking amongst ourselves, including Jess when possible, though of course he never responds.

"We'll be back this afternoon," I tell Jess.

Gary and Ian agree.

As we walk down the hall, a man of our age comes from the other direction, several books in his hand. It's one of those faces—hardened, rough, a little too pink maybe, red almost, but then he's just come into the warmth of the hospital out of the freezing cold. He's a big guy, strong and only a bit overweight. He looks familiar and it occurs to me I might have met him at work—there are a hundred guys at the warehouse who look like him, but that isn't it. Maybe the army? And what the fuck's he doing here—

"Iggy!" I blurt out. "Iggy Barnes!"

It stops him cold. He eyes us suspiciously, gaze going from me to Gary to Ian. The tension mounts. The man might just explode. I clench my fist and cock my arm, preparing to use the haymaker. A grin spreads over Iggy Barnes' face.

"The douche-bags!" he declares.

We don't know what to say to that.

He slaps our shoulders and elbows us like we're long-lost relatives.

"I remember you assholes," Iggy declares. "Fuckheads." Suddenly, his face goes dark. "I know what you're doing here." He looks away like he can't stand the sight of us anymore.

I tense up again.

Then Iggy sort of collapses into one of the chairs. He looks like he might actually cry, this big monster/killer of a man.

"What are *you* doing here?" I ask him.

He doesn't answer.

"Iggy?" I try again.

Ian and Gary and I wait for Iggy's answer. I'd really like to get him alone to talk to him. I worry he's going to blurt it all out how he'd found that orange-and-white-striped shirt in his backpack. I worry Ian and Gary are going to put it together that Iggy and Officer Hank had history, instigated by *me*, and the assault with the iron barwasn't just some random act of mayhem on Iggy's part. I worry *I* killed Officer Hank—*me*—when you get down toit. Inadvertently...but still.

Iggy fingers the books. They're old books, hardbacks from the library, or maybe bought on the internet. Then I see it, the big book on the bottom, our old high school yearbook. I look for a place to run to and hide.

"I come here to read to Jess," Iggy explains. "He likes mysteries and thrillers. I don't know if he can even hear me, but I figure 'why not?' I like reading and I'm getting into the books, so even if it's not doing him any good, it's good for me. I need to pay off my debt to the guy—I owe him big time."

We still don't understand. Iggy can see that on our faces.

"Jess wrote to me halfway through my first year of incarceration," he explains.

"He was the one who called the cops that night and told them I killed that police officer." Iggy grabs a breath. "Officer Hank."

We all look at each other.

"Jess told you that?" I ask in disbelief. "He told you he called the cops on you."

"In that very first letter," Iggy says. "At first I wanted to kill your friend, but as the years went by, I realized he'd done me a big favor really. When I hit that Officer Polensky, I was lost and angry and just about to murder my mother and her new boyfriend, swear to God. I was bound to do it the next day or the day after that. Anyway, I was convinced he'd saved me by dropping that dime on me. And he kept writing to me, which was fucking brave. It showed he really gave a fuck what happened to me. Nobody else had ever done that before."

We're stunned. We don't know what to say.

"Now you remember this, I bet," Iggy says, pulling the yearbook out from under the bottom. "We look at the pictures and I talk about what I remember about each of the students." Iggy opens the book to a page as if by magic and points to a picture of me and Jess and Ian and Gary running around the ballfield, doing laps, together in a pack like we always were. The page is signed by all of us, with some filthy, sarcastic remarks which refer to things I don't recall now. And I'm wearing the orange-and-white-striped t-shirt—

Iggy and I catch eyes. I look away and don't dare look up again. I touch the yearbook photograph and cover the image.

"For me, those years were hell," Iggy says. "For you, according to Jess, the best years of your lives."

We let that linger for awhile.

"All these years," I finally tell Iggy, "Jess never told us anything. He never told us he was the one who gave you up. He never said he was still in touch with you."

"So maybe you didn't know him as well as you thought," Iggy smiles.

"That's for sure," Ian agrees.

"The little bastard," Gary chimes in.

We all laugh now, with only a touch of bitterness.

"So, when I got out," Iggy goes on, "I got my parole switched here to Colorado, and Jess got me a job washing dishes at one of the resorts. He was already a big shot, teaching hot, ball-sucking vacationers how to ski and taking them down the river in rafts. I tell you, that Jess got so much pussy..."

Iggy exhales, a whistle really.

A moment of silent respect follows.

Iggy's face darkens again.

"I know why you're here," he says again, circling back to the beginning. "Jess told me all about your little 'pact.' He even wanted *me* to swear I'd kill him."

"What did you say?" I ask.

"I told him to go fuck himself."

I nod. Sounds about right. I study Iggy's face. He's a year or two older than me; back in school there was no way I could kick his ass in a fair fight. Now things are different—a year or two older is a *disadvantage*, not an advantage. But then again, he'd been to prison. *Had that hardened him? Or had it defeated him—taken the air out of his sails?* Little of both, I guessed.

"Now get the fuck out of here and don't come back, understand?" Iggy declares. "I won't let you do it."

"We promised," I tell him with as much conviction as I can muster. I'm not in love with the pact, but I don't like being told what *not* to do, not by the likes of Iggy Barnes, no matter how reformed he appeared to be on the surface.

"Yeah, yeah," Iggy scoffs. "You pansies are gonna kill a guy. Don't make me laugh."

I can take him; I decide in a moment of revelation. *I can beat the living crap out of Iggy Barnes.* And I want to, desperately. Maybe it's jealousy—he'd been Jess's friend all these years when the rest of us weren't —

"Where you guys staying?" Iggy asks.

Why the hell do you wanna know that? I wonder. *You gonna invite us to crash with you?* I picture a blue-tarp homeless encampment under a highway bridge somewhere.

Neither Gary nor Ian wants to say. I stick our necks out and tell Iggy the name of our hotel.

"Maybe I'll come by tonight," he says. "Show you some Denver nightspots worth seeing."

None of us think this is a good idea, but we don't say so.

"I'll ask for you at the desk," he goes on. "Don't worry—I know all your names. Jess talked about you douche-bags all the time."

CHAPTER 33 —

There was something funny about the way the car was parked. That's how it started. It was a white Acura, Angie's car really, and she always parked it on the driveway, perfectly, front bumper six inches from the garage door, driver's side wheels a foot from the edge of the pavement next to the grass. Now the car was a foot and a half short of the garage and a foot and half from the grass. And I knew Angie hadn't driven it; she was out of town visiting her mother, who had had some health issues.

Our son Daniel was at college, so I knew it wasn't him, either. Tyler, however, was fifteen years old, with a learner's permit, prohibited from driving alone.

I put my hand on the Acura's hood. It wasn't burning hot, but it was warm. I went into the house. Tyler sat at the dining room table eating a burger and fries from Romaburger's, a hole-in-the-wall three or four miles away. Tyler had a math book open and was working with a pencil on problems in a notebook.

"Romaburger's, huh?" I said.

"Yeah, I was hungry. Since Mom's not here to make dinner, I thought it'd be okay."

"Uh huh. How'd you get there?"

"Rode my bike," he said, and I had to admire the way he said it—cool, without flinching, a born liar.

"You drove the car," I said.

He started to protest—

"You drove the car and I know you drove the car, so just shut up," I growled. "And if you ever do that again, I'm hauling you down to police headquarters to have you locked up for grand theft auto and sent to Juve Hall or maybe the penitentiary. I'm not sure which they do with a kid your age who commits a heinous felony."

Tyler put down his pencil and looked at me skeptically. He didn't need to say a thing. I heard him loud and clear. *"You're going to call the police?"* that look asked. *Mister second-generation mobbed-up Rudolpho Molero "Scotty" Carollo? Going to the police?*

He had me there. I gave him that, and for the first time in Tyler's existence, I realized how much he looked like me. People said that all the time and I never really saw it, but right then I did, and it wasn't a good feeling.

"So maybe not," I change tactics. "Maybe I don't call the cops. Maybe I just take you down to the bus depot and drop you off with twenty bucks and a ticket out of town, 'cause if your mother knew you were a car-thief it'd break her heart. Or maybe I'll strangle you and cut your dead body into little pieces and keep 'em in the freezer in the garage and put 'em down the garbage disposal one piece at a time over the course of a year."

It broke *my* heart, but I could see Tyler believed me that I'd do it, maybe.

"Okay, Dad," he said. "I'm sorry. I won't do it again."

"Okay then."

"I got you a cheeseburger and fries and a Coke," he said. "It's in the kitchen."

"Okay," I sighed, suddenly very hungry.

CHAPTER 34 —

We start drinking in the bar in the middle of the afternoon. It's quickly evident we haven't thought this thing through. First off: how?

"We could smother him with a pillow," Gary suggested.

"You mean pull his oxygen mask off, leaving fingerprints, then smother him with a pillow, then put the mask back on, leaving more fingerprints," I point out.

"Okay, smartass," Gary says. "How would you do it?"

"Pull the plug," Ian says.

"What plug?" I come back. "Which plug? There are lots of plugs. 'Pull the plug' is just an expression, and not very helpful."

"I can find out," Ian suggests, taking out his phone.

"You gonna Google it?" I ask. "'Hey, Siri—How do you kill someone in intensive care?' That won't look suspicious when they investigate—"

"They won't investigate, will they?" Gary asks, panic in his voice.

"Of course they'll investigate," I say.

"People die in the hospital all the time," Gary complains, "especially when they're comatose already."

"They'll investigate," I assure everyone.

"I have VPN," Ian states meekly.

"That won't matter if it's homicide," I say. I'm talking out my ass, but these jokers don't know that. "If it's homicide, they'll have access to everything."

"That's just on TV," Ian snickers. "In real life, nobody's going to give a flying fuck."

"That's right," Gary agrees, two against one now. "We pull one plug at a time and see what happens."

"One of the nurses will come running," I tell them. "He's being monitored constantly."

"Then we have a lookout and plug it back in if it doesn't do the trick," Ian says. "We try different plugs until one of 'em kills him."

"And we're standing there like nothing's going on while there's one power cut after another," I complain.

"I know some doctors," Ian says, scrolling through contact numbers on his phone. "I can ask."

"Don't," I command, covering Ian's phone-screen with my hand, not sure whether to laugh or cry. "How smart is that? Bring in someone else into this? Create another witness against us?"

Neither Ian nor Gary has anything to say about that. Silence rules.

"Okay," Ian says to Gary, "first we get a big burrito dinner for Scotty here—" Ian jerks his thumb at me, "—and send him in there to fart Jess to death."

Gary laughs.

"Yes, yes."

They crack up. I shake my head.

A waiter comes over and we order more drinks. I wonder if the waiter's heard us. Or the bartender. I'm pretty sure they hear lots of things in that bar, and probably don't call the cops, but maybe they aren't above blackmail when the chance arises.

"And let's say we do manage to kill Jess like we promised," I whisper when the waiter's gone, "who's going to keep Iggy Barnes from killing us? You heard him. He pretty much promised he'd do that."

At that point—speak of the Devil—I spot Iggy coming in from the cold and walking across the hotel lobby. I'm the only one who sees him—Gary and Ian's backs are to the entrance—a deadly mistake for an old gunslinger like me.

"Excuse me," I say, "gotta hit the john."

One thing about being a man of our age, nobody questions this quick exit, no matter how many times an hour you pull it.

I intercept Iggy on his way to the front desk and guide him out of the bar's line of sight.

"Ian and Gary are in the bar," I tell him. "I wanted to talk to you alone."

"Good idea."

"Listen, first I gotta apologize," I say, surprising myself. I hadn't planned on that.

"Fuggedaboutit," Iggy jokes, punching me on the shoulder.

"It was me who threw the rotten apple. It was me who got you in trouble with Officer Hank in the first place."

"I know that. I always knew that. Right from the start. You and that orange t-shirt were famous, the stinky old thing."

"You never said anything—"

"The lawyer said not to," Iggy explained. "He said if I told anyone how Hank had taken me in previously and roughed me over for the apple-throwing deal, which I gather was *you*, it showed how there was 'premeditation' and I could get a lot more time. 'Better to keep it an accident,' he said."

I swallowed and nodded.

"Even so," I say, "if it wasn't for me, you and Hank wouldn't have gotten into it that night."

"Yeah well, fuck you for that," he says, "and I mean that sincerely, and fuck your mother, too—like I did last night and three times this morning, once in the ass—"

I have to laugh; I can't help it.

"But you don't control the universe," he goes on. "You don't say what causes what which causes something else. You're off the hook. You don't have any responsibility. Shit happens. What are ya gonna do? Nothin', that's what I say."

I stare in awe. *Couldn't have said it better myself.*

"What are you gonna do?" I shrug.

"Fuggedaboutit," Iggy agrees. "Now about Jess..." Iggy says. "I was a hard ass with you before, but I've changed my mind. You think it's better he goes now instead of waiting around forever—well, I get it. It's what he wanted, and you promised. It's none of my business to get in your way. But I gotta ask you a favor. You gotta promise *me* something."

"What?" I ask, worried it would be another huge pain-in-the-ass deal—that's how I'd gotten into this mess in the first place.

"Don't do it tonight," Iggy says. "Wait till tomorrow. There's a train leaves tonight at 6 pm for the East Coast and I got a ticket. I'll get into a fight and get arrested somewhere in Nebraska, and get thrown in the clink just to prove it wasn't me who did the killing."

"You don't have to do that, do you?" I wonder.

"Absolutely," Iggy replies. "I'm a known killer. I've done it before, and I've done time for it. As a con, it'll all fall on me if Jess dies."

I stare at Iggy and wonder what it's like to be him, always on the run, even when he hasn't done anything. Me, I've done all kinds of things and never faced the consequences.

"There's something else," Iggy says, looking around, making sure no one hears. "Jess bought a house here in town. It's mostly paid for. He made me his beneficiary. If he dies, the house goes to me."

I try to believe that doesn't make any difference, but by the guilt on Iggy's face, I see maybe it does. Hating myself for the thought, hating Iggy even more, I have to admit I wonder now how much the house is worth, and how that value might have influenced Iggy's change of thought on the subject of assisted suicide.

"Okay," I tell Iggy, giving him the benefit of the doubt. "We weren't going back to the hospital till tomorrow anyway. You catch your train. You going back to Oakburgh?"

"Yeah," Iggy sighs. "It'll be weird, huh? It's all changed, I bet."

I nod. I'm not sure. I'm like the frog in the slowly heating water—if Oakburgh's boiling me alive, I haven't noticed yet.

An elderly couple walks into the lobby from the street. There's something familiar about them but I can't place it. They're seventy to eighty years old. The man's in great shape, though, and so's the woman—

"Jess's parents," Iggy says, spotting them at the same moment.

Now I recognize them, especially *her*. I find her even more attractive than ever, even though she's in her seventies.

"I invited them to come over," Iggy says. "They're divorced actually. They live a thousand miles apart, but they came together to be with their son in his last hours."

I look back at Iggy and marvel at the sincere sentimentality of the man. I resist the urge to try the haymaker on him.

We go to Mr. and Mrs. Freeman, and all of us go into the bar to join Ian and Gary. Everybody drinks except for Iggy, who has a Coke. Mr. Freeman tells us how Jess was injured: freak chair-lift accident.

We never thought to ask the specifics, I realize. As non-skiers, we'd just assumed skiing was a dangerous sport that could kill you at any moment.

"Listen, I gotta go," Iggy said, looking at his watch. *"Gotta pack, gotta catch a train,"* was left unsaid.

"Did you know Jess and Iggy were friends?" I ask Mr. and Mrs. Freeman when Iggy's gone.

"Yes, I knew," Jess's mother says. "But it's not so surprising, their relationship. People looked at Jessup and saw someone they could trust and confide in. Someone who would keep his word even if nobody else would."

The way she looks at us, panning across each of our faces—she's daring us to do as we promised, to end her son's life if that life proved to be a burden.

"I can't stand to see Jess the way he is now," Jess's mother confides in us, her lower jaw quivering. She takes a drink to keep from crying. Her ex-husband the Marine puts a hand over her hand. He looks like he's gonna cry too.

CHAPTER 35 —

I gotta do it myself. That's what I decide. Go in and just do it. I don't know exactly *how*; I plan to improvise. Look at the circumstances and come up with something on the spot. Maybe I'll use a pillow, maybe I'll kick out some cords. I'll wing it. The main thing is Gary and Ian don't have to be involved. They're weak. They won't stand a chance under interrogation if it comes to it. They'd die in prison if they had to do hard time. I know people. I'd be okay. Most likely it won't come to that, but Gary showed himself to be a wimp-out long before with the mailboxes. And everyone knows Ian's a coward, just on the basis of how he runs from life and refuses to face it head-on.

So, I go alone, getting up early when I'm sure Ian and Gary are asleep in their room and Iggy is safely a state away on a train. I take my pocketknife with me. I could poke a hole in an IV bag maybe, or a hole in Jess, right in a lung. Or find a junction box and cut power to the room. Keep it a mystery. I hadn't seen closed circuit TVs—visitors didn't have to sign in or out. There's a way, I tell myself. I'd do it quick and get back in my bed at the hotel. *Just let 'em try and figure it out*, I dare the world.

I park a few blocks away on a residential street where an extra car at the curb won't be noticed. I walk to the hospital in the freezing dawn air. I have a hoodie on over my leather jacket, and it's cinched up to cover my face. It's actually not that suspicious; the freezing cold merits the clothing. I hold a pair of sunglasses in my hand. A half block from the hospital I put on the shades.

This early in the morning, it's easy to make my way to Jess's room without anyone questioning my presence. Still, I feel my heart pounding in my chest.

When I get to the little visitor's break room down the hall from Jess's room, I freeze.

Ian and Gary are there.

I'm surprised by their presence; I shouldn't have been.

"What are you douche-bags doing here?" I ask.

"Same thing as you," Ian says.

"Get the fuck outta here," I order.

"No," Gary states simply.

"Did anyone see you? Does anyone know you're here?" I ask.

"We took a cab," Ian says defiantly. "I gave the driver my card—told him any time he was in New Jersey to give me a call."

"You dumb shits," I mutter, and sit down hard. "It's just like you mental defectives to screw things up like this."

"We do this together or we don't do it at all," Gary states.

"You just make that up?" I smirk.

"We're brothers," Ian insists.

"No, we're not," I shoot back. "I have a brother. A *real* brother. His name's Danny."

"You know what he means," Gary spits out angrily.

"It's a pact," Ian joins in, tag-teaming me. "A group effort."

"No individual initiative allowed," Gary volleys.

I sigh. I try to think. I'm both moved and angered by their noble gesture.

"You have a plan?" I ask.

Gary and Ian look to each other. They've obviously talked about this, scheming in private without me, which pisses me off even more. *Where's the "group effort" in that?*

"We're just going to do it," Ian finally says.

"Just do it?"

"We won't try to hide," Gary explains. "Take full responsibility. Mercy killing. A kindness. An act of civil disobedience. Violation of an unjust law. We figure what can they do to us?"

"Put us in prison," I point out.

"First offenders," Ian shakes his head confidently. "Probation at most. A fine."

"We had that other conviction," I say, and wish I hadn't, realizing:

"For throwing rotten apples," Gary chimes in.

"As juveniles," Ian adds.

I stand. I take off my sunglasses and loosen my hoodie, letting it drop, exposing my face to the world.

"Let's do it, then," I say, and head for Jess's room.

It's dark, which is different than when we'd been there before. A funny thing to do, it seems to me—*turn off the lights so the comatose patient can sleep?* I flick the switch and the fluorescents flicker on as bright as daylight.

"Jess, can you hear me?" I ask, leaning in close, talking way too loudly, hoping against hope everyone had been wrong about him ever coming alive. "It's me, your old pals—Scotty, Ian and Gary. Say something. Give us a sign."

We watch. We wait.

"C'mon, douche-bag," I whisper. "Don't fuck around..."

Jess's feet move at the end of the bed!

Gary shrieks sort-of, a girlish whine, not too loud, though.

"What was that?" Ian asks.

I don't know. I can't say. I can't even speak.

Frantically, like a prospector down to his last plate of beans, Gary claws at the end of the bed, unwrapping a tightly wrapped blanket and sheet, pulling them out, exposing a couple of inflatable devices.

"It's to keep his legs from swelling," I tell the others. "They're like balloons. They tighten around the ankles."

"What are you—a doctor?" Gary asks sarcastically.

I laugh. It strikes me as hilarious.

"My grandmother had those after her stroke," I explain, "if it's any of your business, which it ain't. Before she *died*, by the way."

Gary's about to come back, but something else happens—

"Look at his toes," Ian says.

"They're moving," Gary points out.

"Take off those booties," I tell Ian.

Ian does it, pulling them apart, making a God-awful Velcro screech.

We wait. Jess's big toe, the right one, twitches slightly.

Is that anything? We wonder but don't say it out loud.

"It's telling us he's not ready to go yet," Gary whispers.

"The hell it is," I say. "How do you get that from a toe?"

"I just have a feeling, that's all," Gary says.

I wonder how stoned Gary is already this early in the morning.

"Move your toe if you're not ready to die," Ian orders loudly.

Jess's toe moves!

"That's nothing," I scoff. "It doesn't mean anything."

"*Cross* your *right toe* if you want to live," Ian tries.

To our amazement, miraculously, Jess does it!

We whoop and laugh. He does it again, over and over.

"Cross your left toe if Gary's dads are a couple of butt-fucking fairy-boys!" I shout out.

"Hey!" Gary protests.

Jess's toes on the left quiver and cross. We double over and hold our sides, it's so funny.

"Cross your right toe if Scotty's mom is a cock-sucking whore," Gary retaliates.

Ian howls.

"Why you, I oughta," I kid, punching Gary in the arm.

Jess answers, crossing his right toes, the two largest ones. We cheer.

"What's going on in here?" a nurse demands to know, pushing into the room. "What's all this noise?"

"He's coming back!" Ian yells, pointing at Jess's toes, which are trying to wriggle free from the coma somehow.

The nurse stares, covers her mouth, and considers.

"That may be nothing, guys," the woman starts to say—

"Jess," I interrupt, "cross your right toes if you like this nurse."

Jess does it. The nurse watches, fascinated.

"What about broccoli?" I ask.

Jess's left toes go to work, crossing one toe over the other.

"I'll...I'll get the doctor," the nurse stammers, hurrying from the room. "Keep talking to him. Keep talking."

Gary leans in and whispers to Jess: "You remember our pact, Jess?"

We wait. Jess's right toes cross.

"He remembers," Ian comments solemnly.

I speak up: "I say we go ahead and kill the bastard anyway."

"What?" Ian whines.

"We came all this way and went through all that hassle—for what? Finish him off, I say."

"Scotty!" Ian protests.

Gary laughs uncomfortably, pretty sure I'm kidding.

Jess's toes on both sides wiggle like crazy, crossing and uncrossing, dancing the mazurka.

"Okay, all right, I'm just busting your balls," I assure him.

CHAPTER 36 —

We stay another two weeks while Jess gets steadily better. By the third day, he's able to speak and sit up and eat solid food—a "miracle" says the nurses and the doctors. Between me and Ian and Gary visiting him, and his parents, he has plenty of company. After the first week, Iggy shows up as well. He doesn't say where he's been, or what happened to him.

We take a couple days off from harassing Jess to go see Ian's parents in Aspen. The house is beautiful, with a world-class view, and Ian's parents are happy, healthy, and getting old. Actually, it's amazing how much they've grown up in the forty years I've known them.

Jess gets us a complimentary ski-package deal at the resort where he works—lift tickets, skis, boots.

Lan brought his own skis, boots and poles, remember.) We drive up into the mountains every afternoon after visiting the hospital. Ian's a pro; Gary gets pretty good at skiing after just a few days. I don't even give it a try. I'm pretty sure I'd end up like Jess if I did, 'cause shit happens and what are ya gonna do? Nothin', that's what. Fuggedaboutit.

Ian and Gary call me a yellowbellied wimp. I point out I have a family to support—wife, kids, grandkids—and they don't. That doesn't shut them up, but I don't care; I'm happy sitting on the deck of the lodge sipping coffee and hot chocolate and eyeing the women. I imagine what it would be like to live there. Even at my advanced age, I bet I could still get all kinds of pussy.

I call Angie and give her an update. I call my two sons and talk to them for awhile.

Life is sweet, I tell them, and let them know if I'm ever in a coma, or near death, or in great pain, I wanna stay alive every minute I'm entitled to—no short cuts.

I buy Ian and Gary plane tickets, drive them to the Denver airport, and make sure they get on the plane. Then I drive Argo home alone, the way I like it.

The End.

Made in the USA
Middletown, DE
25 March 2025

73273248R00144